3

Morgantown Church of the Brethren
464 Virginia Ave.
Morgantown, W. Va. 26505

New Insights into Biblical Stories

Yeast, Salt and Secret Agents

New Insights into Biblical Stories

Yeast, Salt and Secret Agents

by
Kenneth L. Gibble

The Brethren Press, Elgin, Illinois

Copyright © 1979, by The Brethren Press, Elgin, Ill.
Printed in the United States of America

Cover design by Ken Stanley
Illustrations by Cathy Earhart

Acknowledgments:

"What Shall We Do With the Drunken Sailor" is reprinted with the permission of the Christian Sermon Society, Raleigh, North Carolina. Originally a sermon, it was chosen in 1976 to receive the Society's Sermon of Merit Award and was subsequently published in *Christian Ministry*.

"What's In a Name," "Yeast, Salt and Secret Agents," "Gobble-Uns, Demons, and the Gospel," "The Christian's Guide to Goofing Off," "Love Your Body," and "Making Believe" were all previously published in *Messenger*.

Scripture quotations unless otherwise noted are from the Revised Standard Version of the Bible, copyrighted 1946, 1952, © 1971, 1973 by the Division of Christian Education of the National Council of the Churches of Christ in the U.S.A.

Library of Congress Cataloging in Publication Data

Gibble, Kenneth L   1941-
   Yeast, salt, and secret agents.

   1. Meditations.   I. Title.
BV4832.2.G49   248'.4   79-780
ISBN 0-87178-968-X

Published by The Brethren Press, Elgin, Illinois 60120

To Mother and Dad:
Anna Ober Gibble and Ralph Z. Gibble
who told me the stories of faith
and the stories of their lives
Until, one day, I saw
it was the same *story, after all.*

TABLE OF CONTENTS

INTRODUCTION   11
    My Story, Your Story, His Story   13
I. ONCE UPON A TIME...   17
    What's In a Name   19
    Monument of Despair   25
    What Shall We Do With the Drunken Sailor?   31
    And Out Came This Calf   37
    Jonah and the Worm   43
    What a King Wants...   51
    The Widow of Zarephath   57
    The Search for Home   65
II. AND THE STORY CONTINUES...   73
    Yeast, Salt and Secret Agents   75
    Who Made Me a Judge Over You?   81
    Just As We Are   87
    Gobble-Uns, Demons and the Gospel   95
    Bringing in the... What?   101
    The Christian's Guide to Goofing Off   109
    Love Your Body   115
    Making Believe   121

INTRODUCTION

MY STORY, YOUR STORY, HIS STORY

Miss Rosa and Miss Ella—that's what all the kids called two elderly women who lived in the village not far from my childhood home. Miss Rosa and Miss Ella were unmarried sisters with a love for little children and a special talent which endeared them to kids of all ages.

They were storytellers.

Not just storytellers, but *great* storytellers. Once a week, all the youngsters in the neighborhood were invited to come to their place for story-time. They would read to us from story books, make up stories of their own, and act out the various parts. Story-time also featured a hand puppet, a clown figure, which each week was given to one of the children who would tell a story he or she had made up using the puppet.

I attended story-time at Miss Rosa and Miss Ella's only once or twice. They started it at a time in my life when I was telling myself I was getting "too big" for that sort of thing. I must have been all of nine or ten at the time. How little I knew about the human experience at that tender age. In my innocence I assumed that stories were only for kids. It was not until later I made the startling discovery that stories are meant for all of us, that age has nothing to do with it. And from the perspective of more than a score and half years behind me, I now see that stories are indeed among the most delightful gifts God has for us. In fact, a person who knows no stories, who has no story of his or her own to tell, is someone to be pitied.

This book has to do with stories: my story, your story, and his story—God's story. Because we are God's children, my story and your story touch each other. Furthermore, they are all a part of that larger story of God's way with His creation. It's an old, old story, but an eternally new story too, as new as your story and my story which are still in process.

What happens when stories are told? First of all, there has to be a storyteller. Often the enjoyment of the listeners depends on how much the storyteller enjoys the story being told. All of us have known people who totally lose themselves in whatever story they are telling. It doesn't matter where they heard the story or whether it is a tale about their own or someone else's experience. When *they* tell it, it becomes *their* story. Regardless if it is the first or the one hundredth time they're telling it, the tale comes alive just by the enthusiasm and aliveness they put into it.

Listen to small children as they tell a story. They let their imaginations run wild; their eyes light up; they spread out their arms and use their hands. Fact and fantasy get all jumbled together, but only the adults get disturbed by that. When kids tell stories, they don't worry whether or not there's a "point" to the story. They don't have ulterior motives behind their stories; they aren't trying to sell anyone anything; they don't want to convert someone to their side of the issue; they aren't interested in teaching a moral lesson. Their stories just "are" and that's the charm of them. Mostly what a child is doing while telling a story is simply sharing something in his or her experience that was funny or scary or exciting. And a child won't be hurt or offended if, after the story is through, a listener says, "So what?" To a youngster, no "what" was intended in the first place.

The best stories, the most enjoyable ones, even for adults, are those which do not look for a particular response from the listeners. The best stories are those which allow the listeners the freedom to react any way they like—to laugh or cry or maybe some of both; to clap the hands in delight, or even to yawn in sleepy contentment. What a true storyteller really longs for is to have the listener say: "I liked that story because . . . well, just because." If the story draws people a bit closer together in joy or celebration or sadness or wisdom, that is reward enough. A real storyteller, says Elie Wiesel, wishes neither to teach nor to convince, but to close gaps and create new bonds. He tries to wrest from death certain prayers, certain faces, certain truths, by appealing to the imagination and nostalgia that make us listen when our story is told.

Our story—what is our story? Each of us has an individual story, to begin with. And we begin learning that story when we are very young. Children are fascinated with the real-life stories that their parents tell them. How well I can remember my mother telling us children about events of her own childhood—of life on the farm, of her fright when people known as 'gypsies' appeared in the neighborhood, of guests coming home each Sunday after church for dinner. As she recounted those long past events, I began to grow familiar with them; the names of her childhood friends, of neighbors and teachers, became names I knew. Her stories became my stories too.

Added to these stories were make-believe ones: stories like Goldilocks and the Three Bears, Little Red Riding Hood, and the Gingerbread Man. Then as I grew older, my own personal stories entered the picture. I would come home and share with the family what had happened at school, what took place while I was playing next door. Later on, there were family stories—events in which all of us participated and which we told each other over and over again, usually with laughter and great enjoyment. They became part of our family tradition; outsiders on hearing the stories had no idea what made them so entertaining to us. It was all part of learning our family story, and these family stories became chapters in our individual stories.

You have experienced much the same thing. And as you have grown older, some of the long ago stories aren't all that clear in your mind anymore. You get confused about the details, but that doesn't matter because it's not the details that matter, but the story, and the fact that it's *your* story.

Now part of what it means to be Christian has to do with your stories and my story. Along the way, the stories of the Christian tradition get woven into the fabric of our personal stories. So much so that we cannot really pull them apart. They become part of the warp and woof of our lives. The vocabulary of faith becomes part of our own vocabulary.

The heart of the Christian faith cannot be communicated by words alone, even when those words are organized into formal, rational outlines we sometimes call doctrine or theology. Our faith is a story—a story of God's dealings with men and women of old, of God's continuing relationship with you and me. Fortunate indeed are those children who hear the stories of faith at home—of Daniel in the den of lions, of the Hebrew children in the fiery furnace, of Jonah and his adventures, of Esther the queen, of the Good Samaritan, the lost sheep, the prodigal son. Hearing these stories over and over again, we begin to see a pattern—of God's creation, human rebellion, and then God's acts of love and grace to win his children back to him.

What a mistake we Christians make if we substitute catechisms and commandments for stories and tales. Our faith does not consist of a list of do's and don'ts about life but it is God's continuing story of creation, judgment, and grace. We understand what the story is all about in Jesus Christ, in whom all persons and events, even all history and creation, have their focus. To become a believer is to accept our place within the story of God's purpose, the story the church tells as a way of experiencing its own identity, the story we tell as the "story of our lives."

That's what this book is all about. In the first section the Old Testament is our focus. We will look at some well-known and some not-so-well-known stories. Our purpose will be to enjoy them, to hear God's challenge through them, and to see our own stories mirrored in them.

In the second section of the book the focus shifts to the impact that Jesus Christ has on our own stories. We will look at issues and problems of daily living and discover resources in the stories of faith for dealing with them.

Warren F. Groff, in his book entitled *Story Time,* makes the point that the story of faith will remain distant and incomplete to us until we make it truly our own by living it and telling it in our own way. The story invites our paraphrase. And as a demonstration of such a paraphrase he offers one of his own:

> Before it all began there was the Storyteller
>   before anyone ever said, "Once upon a time"
>   before characters, plot and story line
>   before galaxies, Milky Way, and any planet's birth
>   before sun and moon and spaceship earth.
>
> The Storyteller loved stories, so
>   he created persons
>   to hear them
>   to tell them
>   to live them
>   to create them.
>
> (From *Story Time* by Warren F. Groff, The Brethren Press, Elgin, Illinois.)

How would you tell the story? How *do* you tell your stories: Your family stories and Bible stories and personal stories? We need to tell them to each other and we need to listen to each other because often we discover the meaning of them, and of ourselves, in the telling.

My story, your story. Each one the same and each one different, but each needing to be heard and told again and again. And encompassing all our stories is *his* story—God's story of promise and fulfillment in Jesus Christ.

It's a good story.

I.
Once upon a time ...

WHAT'S IN A NAME

Shakespeare said it. Or at least he wrote it. He wrote it in a play called "Romeo and Juliet," and the words are renowned:

> What's in a name? That which we call a rose
> By any other name would smell as sweet.

Now with all due respect to the Bard of Stratford, I happen to believe that names do matter—that they have significance in the realm of faith—even (and here I hesitate, because the idea may strike you as preposterous) that in having names and giving names and naming names, we come into loving, intimate touch with the very being of God.

Getting us started on this exploration are the opening words of a song which Jim Croce helped make popular just a few years ago:

> Like the pine trees lining the windin' road,
> I got a name,
> I got a name,
> Like the singin' bird and the croakin' toad,
> I got a name,
> I got a name,
> And I carry it with me like my Daddy did . . .
> ("I Got a Name," C. Fox, N. Gimbel. From the film, "The Last American Hero," Fox Fanfare, Inc.)

For some reason those words grab me every time I hear them.

They remind me of that fascinating story in Genesis where Adam is in Eden, the beautiful garden; and the Lord God brings to him every beast of the field and every fowl of the air "To see what he would call them; and whatever the man called every living creature, that was its name" (Gen. 2:19).

Thus, the singin' bird and the croakin' toad receive their names, so that then—and only then—is the act of creation completed. And is this not true in human experience—that neither a person nor a thing is real, is created, until it has a name? To have the privilege of naming is to receive one of God's gifts. It is to be God's partner in creation.

To be able to name something is also to have some control over it. You are feeling ill; you go to your doctor. Only after you are examined, only after your doctor has been able to diagnose and give a *name* to your sickness, can any steps be taken to control it and cure it.

During my days as a seminary student, I spent one day each week as a substitute teacher in Chicago high schools. It was there I learned what power the naming of names can have. On those occasions when I walked into a classroom with no means of identifying the students, I had little chance of establishing any kind of control. To say to the fellow at the back of the room: "You in the dark pants and red shirt, take your seat," was to indulge in an exercise of futility. But what a difference when a provident teacher had left on the desk a seating chart for me. Then I could look directly at the offender and say with confidence, "Joseph Kovacevic, take your seat."

To be able to say the name is to exert a certain power over the person being named. Maybe that is why the very anonymity of a crank letter or crank phone call adds to the terror. If we cannot name our adversary, we are completely at the mercy of a poisonous mind. How can we confront an enemy who is nameless?

Names are important for other reasons as well. Our names represent us; they distinguish us from other people. So we naturally resent it when someone addresses us as "Hey You" or "What's Your Name." We feel dehumanized when governments and businesses identify us by number rather than by name. We get irritated when we see our names misspelled or hear them mispronounced.

Even worse is the sense of violation we feel when someone abuses the gift of name-giving. A person asking you for your name is asking for a great privilege. For you to answer by giving your name is risky. You are entrusting yourself to a stranger. And sometimes the result can be unpleasant.

I recall an occasion when a salesman asked for a few minutes of my time. Like most people, I tend to be wary of those who want to sell me something; so after agreeing to listen to him, I became even more apprehensive when he began by asking: "What's your name?" Reluctantly, I told him. It was a mistake, for no doubt in one of his training courses this man had been told that if you can get on a first-name basis with a prospect, you're half-way home. And so he said, "Well, Ken, I have something here I know you'll be interested in."

And I tell you—if he had been giving away 100-dollar bills, I would not have been interested. He had violated a sacred trust. I had given him my name and he had abused it by claiming an intimacy that did not exist.

Names are to be handled with care. Nicknames can hurt a child if they are given in ridicule, but they can also be a wonderful affirmation if they grow out of respect or affection. Jesus gave Simon the nickname of Peter or "Rock" because he saw rocklike qualities in him. God changed Jacob's name to Israel because of his perseverance.

Those whose names were changed from Bobby to Bob, from Susie to Sue, from Billy to Bill, will remember that the name symbolized and even helped bring about a change in who they were. When I let it be known that I had outgrown "Kenny" and was ready to be called "Ken," I pretended not to see my parents' faces as they vainly tried to conceal their amusement. I also had to endure the forgetfulness of grandparents, aunts, and uncles, who kept calling me "Kenny" long after everyone else had laid that childhood name to rest. Occasionally I'll run into a long-time family friend who hasn't seen me in years. I hope they can forgive my smile when I hear them say: "How are you, Kenny?" I'm smiling because I realize that to them I'll always be the youngster by that name.

And that's okay, for all of us love to hear our names spoken with warmth and affection. Exchange of names—especially first names—draws us together. One of the features of my own church I most appreciate is the emphasis on mutuality. If a member of the church receives recognition in the community and obtains a title such as "Reverend" or "Doctor," that makes no difference to the church. Within the congregation that member is still "Brother Miller" or "Sister Bucher."

Perhaps the designation of "brother" and "sister" sounds strange to our ears these days. But using each other's given names is a way of showing mutual respect from oldest to youngest, and it is also a way of expressing affection. Names are important in helping us become the community of Christ.

Central to the Christian faith is the belief that each of us is known—individually—by our Creator. God knows us by name. The New Testament symbol for this is the imagery of the Book of Life on whose pages are written the names of the faithful (Revelation 21:27).

Somehow the beauty and meaning of that image is shattered if we picture a giant stack of computer print-outs. The Book of Life contains no numerical codes. Our *names* are *written* there.

What about the name of God? Most of us grew up being taught that profanity was wrong, that to swear was to incur the divine wrath. The words of the third commandment are plain enough: "You shall not take the name of the Lord your God in vain" (Exodus 20:7).

I believe that commandment is as important today as it was when it was first given thousands of years ago. But my reasons for thinking so have changed.

To explain, I go back to a story from my early school days.

There were just three of us in the first grade class of our one room school: Miriam Cassel, Mark Bauman, and myself. As first graders, we were given special privileges by our teacher, Elizabeth Gibbel—one of which was an occasional recess when the weather was pleasant.

On this particular day, we were enjoying the exercise which the swings and see-saws provided when somehow or other, we became embroiled in a moral issue of profound consequences. Each of us came from church-going families, and so we knew a thing or two about SIN. At least we had heard there was such a phenomenon, and we had been told it was something we would do well not to indulge in. A case in point was bad language. One of us therefore raised the question: "Is it wrong to say "Holy Cow" or "Holy Mackerel?"

As I recall, we were divided on the issue. One of us had heard—no doubt from an adult—that such expressions were frowned on. Maybe using such words wasn't SIN, but it came mighty close.

"But what makes it wrong?" one of us wanted to know. It could be the dissenter had felt a stab or two of guilt—or at least a gentle twinge. Because it was certainly true—undeniably true—that in the heat of playground excitement, we had each of us cut loose with an occasional "Holy Mackerel." Or even, when emotions reached a fevered pitch, "Holy Moses!" What *did* make it wrong? we wanted to know.

After lengthy debate, the truth came to us. The fact was neither mackerels nor cows were sacred things. Therefore, it must be wrong to call something holy that was not holy. We resolved that henceforth, if we felt a need to express enthusiasm, we would resort to phrases like "Holy Bible" or "Holy Ghost." We were sure that Moses also was holy, even though he was in a slightly different category.

Children certainly have a way of getting things turned around, don't they? Or is it adults who get things turned around? The more I reflect upon that childhood experience, the more I am convinced that we youngsters were fundamentally right. Sometimes the perceptions of children cut through the hang-ups and the hypocrisy that so plague grown-ups.

No longer do I believe God is offended or angered when his name is thrown around as slang. Can any of us seriously believe that the Almighty's dignity could be injured by the words we utter?

It is not God whom we hurt when we take God's name in vain; it is ourselves. The third commandment does not exist to protect God's holiness, but to protect us from ourselves.

There come moments in life when we are touched deeply—perhaps by grief, or by joy, or fear, or by a deep feeling of relief that a dreaded thing has not come to pass. At such moments, we do not—or cannot—speak in long, carefully crafted sentences. Instead, from deep inside us come words which are a cry or a prayer or some of each. And we may exclaim: "Oh my God!" "Oh Christ!"

That is not profanity. It is faith. It is naming the name beyond which one cannot go.

But how can we name that name if we have used it as part of casual conversation? What does the person who says "Oh my God" twenty times a day say when confronted by a moment of truth? I don't know. But it may be that such a moment is a judgment passed on those who have used the divine name lightly. Likewise, that lack of faith can also be explained by those whose conversation is too-generously sprinkled with "Praise the Lord."

We would do well to pay more attention to names: to the name of God, to the names of our acquaintances, to the names of our loved ones, to our own names.

What's in a name? A lot more than we supposed at first thought. For "like the singin' bird and the croakin' toad, you and I got a name." We carry it with us and it is known by God.

MONUMENT OF DESPAIR

There is a man in the book of Genesis with the interesting name of *Lot*. We will also give attention to his wife. The scripture says:

> Lot's wife behind him looked back, and she became a pillar of salt (Gen. 19:26).

That's some way to make it into the pages of scripture, isn't it?

But before we can come to any kind of understanding of this woman, we must take a fresh look at the story of her husband, Lot.

At the outset I must confess that I find it difficult to like all of the men and women we meet in the Bible, not just the bad ones, but even some of the good ones. David, for example. I know he's one of the great heroes of the faith; but for some reason or other, I have never been able to come to a genuine liking of him.

What may be even more reprehensible, I find that I do have a liking for some of the "bad guys" in the scriptures. Or, if not a liking, then at least a certain sympathy. I've always felt, for instance, that Jezebel, that wicked queen, got something of a bad press by the writers of scripture. But among the supposedly "good guys" of the Bible, I find this person named Lot one of the most disgusting of all. To be sure, Lot certainly does not qualify as a saint. The stories about him are clear enough about this. And yet he is considered one of the faithful, a member in good standing of the people of God.

Lot's chief claim to fame is his blood relationship to the father of the faith, Abraham himself. Knowing this, I suppose I should try to be more understanding of Lot. It is a dubious blessing to be related to a famous person. You suffer the indignities of being a public figure and you obtain none of the rewards. What must it be like to be a brother of a president, to be the son or daughter of an entertainment celebrity, to be the husband or wife of a renowned intellectual? You will likely never be known or appreciated or accepted for yourself. For the rest of your life you will live in the bright glory and the dark shadow of that famous one.

Lot was Abraham's beloved nephew. The time comes for Abraham to divide the grazing land between himself and Lot. The two of them go up to the mountain where they can see for miles around. Abraham, generous and gracious as befits the father of the faith, gives his nephew a choice. The land to the east is green and well-watered, a perfect place for a man's flock. The land to the west is poorer in every respect. Naturally Lot chooses the fertile land to the east.

"And why not?" you say. "Abraham gave him the choice, didn't he?"

Yes, of course he did. Lot's decision does not satisfy my sense of justice, even though Abraham seems not to have been bothered by this turn of events. At least the text makes no mention of it. Had I been he, I would have fumed inwardly. I can hear myself muttering: "So this is the thanks I get for taking care of my brother's son all these years."

But my disgruntlement at Lot's choice merely exposes my foolishness. For had I been there and tried to shame him by saying: "You have a nerve, to choose the fertile land," Lot would have replied:

"Uncle, had *I* given *you* the choice, what portion would you have taken for yourself?"

I would have answered, "I know what is fitting. I take the land to the west and leave the fertile eastern fields for you, my kinsman."

And Lot would have answered, "Then you have no complaint. For that is exactly how the matter now stands. You have the western lands, I the eastern."

To be sure, our good opinion of ourselves frequently betrays us.

But at the very least we can agree that Lot was a bit on the selfish side. And that's not the worst of it. It isn't long after he moves east that he takes up residence in that city of legendary wickedness, Sodom. The tellers of this ancient narrative had a bias against city life. Just like many in our own day, they thought of the city as a cesspool of dirty streets and rampant immorality. Sodom was, for them, a symbol of the evil that both terrified and fascinated people. And this attitude toward the city is still with us. You come across it in conversations, read it in editorials, and hear it in campaign speeches of politicians. Down with the wickedness of the city! Up with good clean country living. "Thank God I'm a country boy!"

Being a product of the country myself, I cannot help being disgusted by the great enthusiasm with which Lot embraces life in Sodom. Lot strikes me as the perennial adolescent. Not rich or famous or fashionably immoral himself, he likes to hang around people who are. He's a "groupie." You see him rubbing elbows with the jet set at the cocktail parties. They ignore him, snub him deliberately, but he doesn't seem to care. He gets his kicks just being this close to decadence. He's terrified by it, yet drawn to it by some irresistible pull. He loves the noise, the color, the blatant sexuality of it. He knows he doesn't belong there, but he knows he can't tear himself away.

And isn't that just the way it is with whatever lust appeals to you and me? Maybe it is money. Maybe it's power. Maybe it's a well-nursed hatred. Maybe it's booze or gossip. We are alternately repelled by them and pulled toward them. And a part of our mind is always ready to savor the fantasies of them. Thank God no one can read our minds at such times!

And so you and I join Lot in Sodom and we, too, stare at the bright lights. That's why we may be properly disgusted with Lot. He is that part of us we find disgusting in ourselves, sometimes to the point of nausea.

But what is this? Abraham enters the picture again. It seems God has been hearing rumors about two wicked cities. He tells Abraham:

> Because the outcry against Sodom and Gomorrah is great and their sin is very grave, I will go down to see whether they have done altogether according to the outcry which has come to me; and if not, I will know (Genesis 18:20-21).

Now understand that this is a very early faith picture of God. In the account we read that God is standing there with Abraham and the two of them are talking face to face. And God tells Abraham that he must investigate the bad reports he's been hearing. Instead of the all-knowing God we read about in most of the scriptures, here we have a God who has to go and see if things really are as bad as people are telling him.

If they *are* that bad, so much the worse for Sodom and Gomorrah. It will be fire and brimstone time—so God tells Abraham.

Abraham intervenes. His nephew lives in Sodom. Suppose God finds 50 good people there; will he save the city on their account? The Lord agrees. But Abraham is just getting started. How about for 45 good people? Yes. How about 40 . . . 30 . . . 20 . . . ten? And the Lord agrees to it. Abraham must have been a persuasive fellow.

Two men enter the city of Sodom. They are really God's emissaries, but they give the appearance of ordinary men. Who should meet them but our friend, Lot. He invites them to be his guests, and when they at first politely decline his invitation, he insists on it. For all his shortcomings, Lot is the perfect host.

Perfect to a fault, we can say. For now the text paints a picture of incredible bestiality. The men of the city have seen the arrival of the two travelers. They surround the house of Lot, demanding that he send out his two guests. The scripture implies that their intent is to give vent to desires that have made the city of Sodom a word still synonymous with depravity (Genesis 19:4-7). Lot is appalled. By oriental custom he has a sacred duty to protect guests who have eaten at his table. He even offers to send out his two daughters to satisfy the desires of the ravenous mob. Needless to say, that offer does little to endear him to us. But no harm comes of it; the crowd wants the two male guests, they're not interested in Lot's daughters.

That this terrible tale is in the Bible is difficult for us to accept. But the truth is that Sodom is a wicked, wicked city. There are not even ten good people to be found. It must, it shall be destroyed.

Only Lot and his family are to be saved. The two emissaries urge them to leave. And the Bible says that Lot "lingered, so the two men seized him and his wife and his two daughters by the hand, the Lord being merciful to him, and they brought him forth and set him outside the city" (Genesis 19:16).

That should be no surprise. Lot has to be dragged, kicking and screaming, as it were, out of the wicked city. And sometimes it is the very mercy of God that drags us out of whatever thing to which we have been enslaved. At the time it does not feel much like a mercy. Only later, older and wiser, do we see that that's what it was all along.

"Flee to the hills," the two men say to Lot. And now give your attention again to the tradition. Lot says:

> Oh no, my lords; behold your servant has found favor in your sight, and you have shown me great kindness in saving my life; but I cannot flee to the hills, lest the disaster overtake me and I die. Behold, yonder city is near enough to flee to, and it is a little one. Let me escape there—is it not a little one?—and my life will be saved! (Genesis 19:18-20).

Of all the speeches in the entire Bible, this is surely one of the most pathetic. Dragged out of one city that is only moments away from fiery destruction, Lot pleads to be taken to another city—"just a little one." And now we see to what extent he and we become enmeshed in evil. We think we cannot live without it. We don't want to overdose on evil. But please, Lord, give us just a little of it to keep life interesting. Why will we persist in the belief that evil is somehow more interesting than goodness? God only knows. And only God can save us from it.

But now, finally, we come to that well-known and fantastic part of the story. As the fire falls from heaven and consumes Sodom, the Lord's emissaries say to the fleeing family, "Do not look back."

> But Lot's wife behind him looked back, and she became a pillar of salt.

I've sometimes felt that Lot's wife was given a bad deal. After all, it was her home she was leaving. She would never see it again. I can't imagine leaving a place where I had spent a significant part of my life without turning around for one last, loving, lingering glance.

Then again, maybe she was reacting to the order that forbade her to look back. If someone tells you to "close your eyes and don't look," you know how great the temptation is to do just the opposite.

But it was not for these reasons that Lot's wife was turned to salt. Her sin was no different in kind from that of men and women in every age. Lot's wife looked back in despair. Lot's wife denied faith. And this is the thing that is beyond saving, even by God himself.

Lot with all his weaknesses—his selfishness, his adolescent cravings for excitement, all of it—Lot can be forgiven. If he wants forgiveness.

But to deny faith, to say "no" to hope and to love, to refuse to trust God and each other, to steadfastly choose emptiness and self-pity and despair—that is to choose death. There are waste-places on our earth that are like the wasteland of a scorched Sodom. And yes, Lot's wife was turned to salt; and many still are turned to lifeless pillars whose salt tears of despair seem permanently frozen on their blank faces.

And here is the truth of it: faith is not a commodity one can have or not have as one chooses. Faith is the essence of our being. Faith is that bond between ourselves and God. It is the thing that links us to all men and women on earth.

That is what we must learn from the monument of despair that was once Lot's wife. To deny faith is to dwell in death—everlasting death. The word of God which we must hear is this: "Therefore, choose life."

Choose life!

WHAT SHALL WE DO WITH THE DRUNKEN SAILOR?

The story of Noah and the flood is a strange story—strange in the telling—how one man and his family take with them into a big clumsy boat a pair of animals of every kind, how the rains come and the rivers overflow and everything becomes one vast, forbidding, death-dealing, watery chaos. How the Lord God preserves Noah's family and brings them to land to propagate the earth, to begin the human experiment all over again.

It is a strange story, strange in its multiplicity. For there is not just one flood story, but many. Nearly every ancient civilization has some tradition or other of a great flood which destroyed every living thing. And the biblical record is not the only one to say that divine intervention was the chief cause of the deluge.

A strange story—strange in what we have made of it in recent times. For to us, there is something dark and primeval about it all, like Prometheus chained to the rock, like Jacob wrestling with his nocturnal adversary on the river bank. In our imagination (for such things are beyond the ken of human memory), we go back to a time when men and gods walked the earth together, when the darkness held unnameable terrors, when monsters roamed the forests and lurked in deep oceans. It is the time of mankind's childhood, filled with the haunts and hobgoblins of childhood. And we remember our own childhood's dark fears, not in our conscious recollection, but in the deep recesses of unconscious, frightful remembering.

And maybe that is why we sophisticated, twentieth-century adults take the forbidding story of Noah and the flood and turn it into a children's story, a children's song. "Old Noah he built himself an ark," we sang as grade schoolers, "there's one more river to cross; he built it all of hickory bark, there's one more river to cross." And so the verses run in this nonsense song, written by an adult, no doubt, who preferred not to let his mind dwell on the image of flood waters rising, inexorably rising.

We do the same to other terrors of our existence. We joke about disease and drunkenness and death to protect ourselves from their hold on us. We reduce the horror of prison camps to the rollicking adventures of Hogan and his heroes. We take the murderous characters of two outlaws and transform them into a delightful duo of technicolored Butch Cassidy and the Sundance Kid. And the monsters that stalked our childhood dreams; these we have dressed in silly costumes and locked inside a noisy box to entertain the kids on Super Saturday's cartoon extravaganza.

This is no new thing—to handle life's anxieties by reducing them to laughable, and therefore manageable size. We *must* do it, sometimes, or the terrors would overwhelm us. And so Bill Cosby tells us that Noah was somewhat reluctant to start hammering boards together until the Lord thundered: "Noah, how long can you tread water?"

And in Marc Connelly's great play, *The Green Pastures,* Noah and God are making plans for getting the animals into the ark.

> *Noah*—Think you'd like snakes, too?
> *God*—Certainly, I want snakes.
> *Noah*—Oh, I kin git snakes, lots of 'em. Co'se some of 'ems a little dangerous. Maybe I better take a kag of likker, too?
> *God*—You kin have a kag of likker.
> *Noah*—Yes, suh, day's a awful lot of differ'nt kin's of snakes, come to think about it . . . water mocassins, cotton-moufs, rattlers. . . . Maybe I better take two kags of likker.
> *God*—I think de one kag's enough.
> *Noah*—No. I better take two kags. Besides I kin put one on each side of de boat, an' balance de ship wid dem as well as havin' dem for medicinal use.
> *God*—You kin put one kag in de middle of de ship. . . .
> *Noah*—Yes, Lawd, but you see forty days an' forty nights—
> *God*—One kag, Noah.
> *Noah*—Yes, Lawd. One kag.

We smile at this, and that is all right so far as it goes. Only it usually goes no further, and there is the rub. As Frederick Buechner writes:

> . . . for all our strategems, the legends, the myths persist among us, and even in the guise of fairy tales for the young they continue to

embody truths or intuitions which in the long run it is perhaps more dangerous to evade than to confront.

All these old tales are about us, of course . . . that is why we can never altogether forget them; that is why, even if we do not read them any more ourselves, we give them to the children to read . . . because if (the stories were lost), part of the truth about us would be lost too. (From *The Hungering Dark* by Frederick Buchner, Seabury Press, New York.)

The story, then, is about a flood. As such it is a story of chaos, of sin and destruction and death. It is about our old childhood terror of death by drowning, of dark days and unceasing rain and water that rises and gathers force and sweeps everything away. The words of Genesis paint a fearsome picture:

> The waters rose and swelled greatly on the earth. . . . The waters rose more and more on the earth so that all the highest mountains under the whole of heaven were submerged. The waters rose fifteen cubits higher, submerging the mountains. And so all things of flesh perished that moved on the earth (Genesis 7:18-21, Jerusalem Bible).

A story about a flood, a true story in the deepest sense of that word. But a story also about Noah, and thus a doubly true story, for it is thereby a story about us.

Noah, the Bible says, found favor in the eyes of the Lord. There was reason for it, because Noah was a good man, a man of integrity.

There's that word: integrity! A human trait all too rare among the children of men; a characteristic Webster defines as "sound, undivided." Or, as we put it in our contemporary language: "having it all together." A man or woman with integrity has learned to know himself, herself. People with integrity are fair and honest in their dealings. Noah had integrity. Noah found favor in the eyes of the Lord.

For then, as now, integrity was not a plentiful commodity. Why is that, I wonder. Maybe because other human traits seem to have greater value in the market place. Style, for example, and charisma (whatever that is). And imagination and diplomacy. But integrity . . . ? And thus it has ever been.

It was not so odd then, that God should favor Noah, a good man. Not only then, not only in ancient Greece when the cynic Diogenes crept through the city with his lantern, looking for an honest man; not only then, but in every time have the Noahs been scarce among us. And so when the Lord from Genesis says, "God regretted having made man on the earth," we are not surprised at that. Not at all.

There is enough slander and cheating and violence in our world to make us all ashamed of our kinship with humanity sometimes.

And so it's almost a relief to walk, in our imaginations, up the gangplank with Noah into that noisy, animal-smelly ark. Oh yes, it's on board we see ourselves. Not out there on the ground as the sky blackens and the raindrops start pelting down. Granted, we may not be as good as Noah was, but at least we're good enough people to be in his league, to be in the same boat, so to speak. And it's certainly too bad for those outside, but well . . . they got what they deserved, we guess. And anyway life on the ark is no picnic, no indeed. Not with Noah's sons squabbling and Noah's wife nagging and some beast or another always rocking the boat.

But at last the waters subside, the land emerges once more, and the good man Noah sends out a dove. And she returns, Praise God! with a fresh green olive twig in her beak. The horror is over; Noah and his family and their unruly passengers thankfully disembark. And while the smoke and incense of Noah's grateful sacrifice ascend to the heavens now turning bright and blue as on the first morning of creation, the Lord God gives his promise:

> Never again will I curse the earth because of man. Never again will I strike down every living thing.

And then, as the humans and the creatures stand on legs still rubbery from their strange voyage, the Lord God draws his bow of many colors across the sky and says,

> This is the sign of the Promise I have established between myself and every living thing that is found on the earth.

And so might the story well end, we think, for has not the good man received his due award, and the evil ones been punished? And here is our mistake. We forget that this is not a fairy tale, but rather a story about us, and therefore a true, an undeniably true story.

The tradition says,

> Noah, a tiller of the soil, was the first to plant the vine. He drank some of the wine, and while he was drunk he uncovered himself inside his tent. Ham, Canaan's ancestor, saw his father's nakedness, and told his two brothers outside . . . and Noah said: "Accursed be Canaan."

And so Noah, the man of integrity, the good man, shows his true colors at last. A good man he may be, but foolish too. A man of faulty

judgment, certainly. A man, when you get down to the fine points, who has both good and evil within him. And that is why his story is our story too.

Like Noah, we take the goodness within us far too seriously, and foolishly think that our own goodness will save us. But then, just when life is booming along beautifully, the other part of us, the dark sinful part, comes to the fore, and we lash out in anger or sink into a depression and we know not why it should be so, but it is so.

For you see, neither Noah nor we can bear the burden of our calling. It is too much to expect of our poor selves, that we reflect the goodness of God, in whose image we were shaped. And so our sinfulness is uncovered, and when it is seen by others—our children, our friends, our coworkers, we may cry out in rage that the fault is theirs . . . for spying on us, for finding us out. "The curse be on you," we shout, thinking thereby to justify ourselves. But it is a foolish pretense, deceiving neither God nor humans.

And so what is to be done with us, with Noah, that good and bad man? How shall the story end?

The old sea chantey asks, "What shall we do with the drunken sailor, earlye in the morning?" And that is the question: what shall we do with that drunken old sailor Noah, who forgot that his goodness was only one part of him? The sailors' song proposed a number of imaginative remedies:

> Put him in a long boat till he's sober . . .
> Hang him by the leg in a running bowline . . .
> Shave his belly with a rusty razor . . .
> Earlye in the morning.

Such remedies may serve, at least for a time. But for the long haul, they will be found wanting, as is true with every punishment.

The truth is that the story of Noah and the flood does not end with: "and they lived happily ever after." The truth is that the story doesn't end at all, but merges into the next story about a tower called Babel and that story leads into another story about a man named Abraham, and the stories go on . . . to tell of a man hung up to die on a cross, and the stories go on . . . and they still go on.

But always there is the promise—now standing out brilliantly in the sky, now barely visible through the gray clouds. Always the divine promise . . . and always the divine mercy. And that is the answer. For whether we are the confident captain standing proudly at the helm or the drunken sailor lying under the table (and we are always some of each), the thing that saves us is the mercy, the divine mercy.

Thanks be to God for that.

AND OUT CAME THIS CALF

I'm really upset with Uncle Henry," the young man complained to his mother. "I'm disappointed with him. You'd think blood would count for something. And me, his only nephew. Why should I stand for such inconsiderate treatment?"

"I don't understand, son," his mother answered. "Your Uncle Henry has done an awful lot for you, you know. When you were a little boy he took you to ball games nearly every weekend. He bought you your first bicycle, invited you to travel with him to a lot of nice places, gave you plenty of spending money. Then when you were ready to go to college, he paid the tuition so you could go to the most expensive university and even bought you a new car each of the four years you attended. And finally, last June, for a graduation gift, he gave you an all-expense-paid tour of the Far East."

"I know, Mother, I know. But what has Uncle Henry done for me lately?"

We've all heard that old story—"What has he done for me lately?"—in one form or another. It's the classic way of reminding us of one of the most predominant failings of human nature—a short memory.

It is part of our humanness to be seldom satisfied with what has been. If a salesman brings in 700 thousand dollars worth of business this year, next year the boss expects him to bring in a million dollars. If their favorite ball player hit 35 home runs this season, the fans next season will be expecting at least 40.

It should come as no surprise to us then, to discover that people have felt the same way about God. This was definitely the case with the people of Israel as they waited impatiently for Moses to come down from Mount Sinai.

The situation was this. Not long before, Moses, by the power of God, had led the people out of their captivity in Egypt. The pursuing armies of Pharaoh had been destroyed. The Lord God had led the people of Israel by pillars of cloud and fire. When they lacked for food, he sent them bread in the wilderness. He provided them fresh water to drink. And he had established his sacred covenant with them, a promise that he would be their God forever. It was at the sacred mountain Sinai that the covenant was given by the Lord, and the mountain shook with thunder, and smoke ascended from its summit to signify the holy presence.

But now that mountaintop experience was a fading memory. Moses, their leader, had been gone for over a month, supposedly in conference with the Lord. The people began to get restless. They started complaining to Moses' brother Aaron, who had been left in charge of things. If Aaron had any spunk at all, he must have reminded them of the many great things the Lord God had done for them in the past. And as he finished his recitation of these events, it probably happened that one of the dissidents destroyed Aaron's entire case with the recurrent question: "Yes, but what has God done for us lately?"

"What ingratitude!" we say to ourselves. Yet if we were a bit more honest with ourselves, maybe we would be reminded instead of our own attitudes. While attending a worship service in which the worship leader was thanking God for all the wonderful blessings of life—the sun, the rain, the beautiful day, the freedom we enjoy as citizens, food to eat, good health, et cetera—I experienced a gnawing feeling inside me which I can only describe as "Yes, but":

"Yes, but I just don't *feel* very grateful right now."

"Yes, but what about all the problems that weigh on my mind?"

"Yes, but what have you done for me lately, Lord?" The truth is we are not much different from those people who came complaining to Aaron.

However, it wasn't only discontentment that brought them to the brother of Moses. Part of what they were feeling was fear. Their leader was gone and rumors were flying. "Moses has deserted us." "Moses has been killed." "We are left all alone out here in the desert." And from these fears an even more devastating thought sprang: "The *Lord* has forsaken us."

Fear works that way. It has transcendent power. We begin by being afraid of something very specific—what we're going to do about a problem at work, for instance—and before we know it, fear takes over our imaginations and we are afraid of losing our job, our health, our family. Until finally we may be reduced to doubting our own sanity, and the wind that blows outside the window in the darkness seems to whisper that the world itself is God-forsaken. Fear has done this to women and men, to you and me, on many a sleepless night.

So perhaps now we can be less harsh in our judgment of the people of Israel when they approached Aaron, the brother of Moses, and said: "Come, make us a god to go at the head of us; this Moses, the man who brought us up from Egypt, we do not know what has become of him" (Exodus 32:1, Jerusalem Bible).

But now the spotlight in the biblical narrative shifts from the people to Aaron. And Aaron is an interesting fellow.

In the first place—and here we can sympathize with him—in this situation, Aaron is in way over his head. He knows it and so does everybody else. There are few more difficult jobs than standing in for the person in charge. Moses was leader—God had chosen him, the Pharaoh had come up against him and been routed, the people had tested him, infuriated him, nearly driven him to distraction. But in the end, Moses had proved beyond a shadow of a doubt that he was in charge.

Aaron had none of this going for him. True, his brother had designated Aaron as his stand-in until he returned. But Aaron simply did not have whatever it took to move the people, to command respect and obedience. We can be reasonably sure he spent most of the time during Moses' absence hoping that the people would not come to him with any demands.

Each of us has been in a similar spot sometime in our lives. I'll never forget how shaky I felt when, as a student teacher, I watched my supervising teacher leave the room for the first time. I knew, and the class knew, and they *knew* I knew, that I was no more in charge than a frog has wings.

That's just about how Aaron must have felt. So it's not at all surprising that, when the people surrounded him and demanded that he come up with a new god, Aaron decided on the spot to give them what they wanted.

Not without a few tugs at his conscience though. We must give him at least this much credit. As the narrative reveals, Aaron knew well enough that to grant the people's request was to commit the sin of idolatry. But despite that awareness—or precisely *because* of that awareness—Aaron comes to us, not as a dim figure in an ancient legend, but as an authentic human being. He is as contemporary as the sun which came up this morning.

This is so because, above all else, Aaron is a rationalizer.

Now it's true that none of us can get along in life without some rationalization. When we are passed over for a promotion, it can be comforting to tell ourselves that all the extra work involved wouldn't have been worth the small raise in salary. In one of Aesop's fables a fox comes upon a bunch of grapes hanging high above his head. After several unsuccessful attempts to pull them down the fox walks away in disgust muttering to himself, "They were probably sour anyway." Whatever else can be said about the fox, one thing is certain—he was far better off convincing himself the grapes were sour than he would have been wearing himself out in futile attempts to pull them down.

So rationalizing *does* have its place. But sometimes we can carry it to questionable lengths as does Aaron. We can almost hear him excusing himself for building the people their golden calf:

> Golly, I don't feel quite right about this, but after all, it will give the people something to do, keep them out of mischief. After all, better to be building a golden calf than to . . . than to . . . Well, I'm sure there are a *lot* of things worse than this. I just can't think of any right now.
>
> Of course, maybe this collecting of gold rings isn't such a good use of the people's possessions. But, after all, taking up a collection, that's at least something *religious,* isn't it?"
>
> Of course, it isn't exactly the kind of religious activity Moses talked about. But, after all, any religion is better than no religion at all. I *think* so, anyway.
>
> Of course, there *is* that second commandment about not making graven images, or bowing down to them. But, after all, don't people need something to believe in they can see with their eyes and touch with their hands? It's just too hard to worship a god who keeps himself hidden, especially when we're out here in the desert. It would be different if we were settled somewhere with a little more security.
>
> Of course, Moses wouldn't stand for this, I'm sure of that. But, after all, I'm not Moses. God surely doesn't expect as much of me as he does of my brother. Besides, these people were wrought up enough to build their own golden calf, even if I hadn't done it for them. This way I can at least maintain some control over things.
>
> Of course, this calf is a real perversion of what our faith should be. Maybe if I can pacify the people for a while, then come up with a good sermon or two, I can have them worshipping the Lord, even if *they* think they're worshipping some other god.

And so it went with Aaron the rationalizer. He even built an altar in front of the golden calf, announced a feast in honor of the Lord God and then tried to convince himself that all the eating and drinking and reveling was worship of Almighty God.

And if you think that is too much to be believed, then I suggest you tune in to some of the religious shows on television these days, with their smartly packaged pop Christianity. The shows are emceed by handsome men with perpetual smiles and a delivery as smooth as the cashmere jackets they wear. From time to time they pause to introduce sleek, sensual females who ooze torch songs to some Robert Redford notion of Jesus. The whole show is done with frequent admonitions to "praise the Lord," and fervent prayers are performed in the best theatrical manner (with the "star" often down on one knee, hands folded).

Whoever the religious huckster may be—and their numbers are increasing rapidly—the end product is always the same: a soft porn version of Christianity, as cheap an imitation of the real thing as was Aaron's golden calf. To support the operation, viewers are invited to send in their gold and silver. You can be sure it too is melted down to build some pretty nifty golden calves. The only thing the people with Aaron had on present-day contributors is that they were close enough to the scene to read the financial report.

Poor Aaron! He wanted so much to believe he was doing the best he could. But no amount of rationalizing could quite remove the feeling of guilt inside. At least he could still feel guilt—and that's something!

Sometimes our own rationalizations are so convincing that we don't feel guilty at all. We say:

> Of course, this item I'm buying may be rather expensive, maybe even extravagant, but, after all, I've worked hard; I deserve it.
>
> Of course, I do have my faults, but after all, I'm not as bad a person as . . . " (insert here the name of the person you usually use).
>
> Maybe my kids are rather spoiled, but, after all, I want them to have it better than I did.
>
> Maybe some of the things I see going on at work do border on the unethical, but, after all, what good would it do for me to speak out against it?

And so it goes, this rationalizing we do. Until, after awhile, our consciences become so jaded we don't even bother to rationalize any more. We just go along. And surely that must come close to what is meant in the Bible by losing our souls.

Only a confrontation with God's word of truth can save us at this point. But very often such a confrontation is a frightening thing, as Aaron himself discovered.

God's word of truth came stalking down the mountain in the form of Moses. Under each arm he carried a stone tablet containing the sacred law. And when he drew near the camp and saw the golden calf standing there and the people dancing round it in drunken frenzy, then—as the *Authorized Version* put it—his "anger waxed hot." He dashed the tablets to the ground and threw the calf into the fire. It is one of the most dramatic scenes in the Bible.

You can imagine how Aaron was feeling all this time. He was wishing he could be any other place than where he was. He desperately tried to remember all those wonderful rationalizations he'd come up with. But when he stood before his brother and tried to explain himself, all that came out was this . . .

> Now Moses, I can explain. It wasn't my fault. You know yourself how bad these people are. They came and insisted I should make them a god; they didn't know what had become of you. So I said, "Who has gold?" And they brought all this gold to me. And I . . . I threw it into the fire and, what do you think? Out came this calf!

And so we see from the story of Aaron and the golden calf that God's word is a scalpel sharp enough to cut through every attempt to deceive ourselves. Yes, it may hurt, but it is a hurting for the sake of good. And when it is God who wields the scalpel, its sharpness may be the only thing that can save us.

"This is going to hurt," says the Great Physician. "But without it, you will remain a victim of your own silly, pathetic attempts to justify yourself."

And that word may be our last, best hope for salvation.

JONAH AND THE WORM

Everybody knows about Jonah and the whale, but hardly anybody knows about Jonah and the worm. It's Jonah and the worm I want you to think about.

> Now the word of the Lord came to Jonah the son of Amittai, saying "Arise, go to Nineveh, that great city, and cry against it; for their wickedness has come up before me." But Jonah rose to flee to Tarshish from the presence of the Lord. He went down to Joppa and found a ship going to Tarshish; so he paid the fare, and went on board, to go with them to Tarshish, away from the presence of the Lord. But the Lord hurled a great wind upon the sea, and there was a mighty tempest on the sea, so that the ship threatened to break up. Then the mariners were afraid, and each cried to his god; and they threw the wares that were in the ship into the sea, to lighten it for them. But Jonah had gone down into the inner part of the ship and had laid down, and was fast asleep (Jonah 1:1-5).

To begin, let's try to get a picture of Jonah. It is a picture with a decidedly modern flavor, because the book of Jonah is a most contemporary book.

To appreciate this description of Jonah, you must realize that he is depicted in the scripture as a rather pathetic, even comical figure. He's one of those fellows who all his life has failed, and yet at the end succeeds so well in spite of himself that he becomes depressed. Failure he had learned to handle; but success?—what do you do with success when you've never had it before?

Jonah reminds me of the leading character portrayed by Art

Carney in the movie, *The Late Show*. He is an aging, disillusioned private detective who has seen better days. Even the better days weren't anything too great, but at least then he didn't have the paunch around the waist or the deep-in-the-chest cough, a 40 year legacy of chain-smoking Camels. Now he's cynical, unapologetically selfish, and not the least bit interested in taking the kinds of chances he once took without a second thought.

This is Jonah: down at the heels, seedy-looking. It has taken years, but he has finally accepted the fact of his insignificance. The years have soured him too; once he may have had visions of being a prophet of stature, the likes of an Isaiah, a Jeremiah. But that was long ago. There have been too many bright promises which burned out early, too many hopes betrayed in the end.

And so when the word of the Lord comes to him to go to Nineveh, the great and wicked city, Jonah behaves just as we would expect such a man to behave. He mutters under his breath: "Who needs this?" and blows town in a hurry. But there's a problem, because when it's the Lord who is doing the recruiting, the Lord often has a policy of not taking "no" for an answer. In this case, at least, Jonah's get-away didn't get him away.

When the storm started throwing the ship around, everyone else got all wrought up about it. They began doing what people everywhere do when things get desperate—they started to pray. Now these prayers weren't made with eyes closed and hands clasped in reverence. Nor was the language of the praying the kind one hears in a Sunday morning liturgy. In fact, the prayers went something like this: "Help!" It is a prayer which should sound familiar to us. Stripped of all refinements, 95 percent of all prayers made to the Almighty consist of that self-same cry.

Where was Jonah while all this was going on? He was below deck sleeping. He knew well enough what the storm was all about. His parents hadn't raised a fool. Soon it would be account-settling time, and that prospect was hardly a joy to contemplate. In the meantime, why not get some sleep? There was nothing else to be done.

> And they said to one another, "Come, let us cast lots, that we may know on whose account this evil has come upon us." So they cast lots, and the lot fell upon Jonah.
>
> Then they said to him, "What shall we do to you, that the sea may quiet down for us?" For the sea grew more and more tempestuous. He said to them, "Take me up and throw me into the sea; then the sea will quiet down for you, for I know it is because of me that this great tempest has come upon you (Jonah 1:7, 11-13).

It could be that when the sailors told Jonah he had won the lottery drawing as the one responsible for the storm, he had two reactions. The first was pleasure: "Gee, I've never won *anything* before this!" The second was resignation: "I should have known better than to think I could run away from *Him*. I might as well take my medicine."

He wasn't even bitter about it. He knew he was getting only what he deserved. Jonah didn't even wait for the crew to suggest the inevitable remedy to the situation. Saving them that unpleasantness, he told them, "Throw me overboard; that should take care of your storm."

So they did, and sure enough, Jonah had been right. And, like many others before and after him, Jonah became immensely well thought-of shortly after his departure.

> And the Lord appointed a great fish to swallow up Jonah; and Jonah was in the belly of the fish three days and three nights.
>
> Then Jonah prayed to the Lord his God from the belly of that fish.
>
> And the Lord spoke to the fish, and it vomited out Jonah upon the dry land. Then the word of the Lord came to Jonah the second time, saying, "Arise, go to Nineveh, that great city, and proclaim to it the message that I tell you." So Jonah arose and went to Nineveh, according to the word of the Lord (Jonah 1:17, 2:1, 2:10-3:3).

It wasn't a whale that swallowed Jonah, after all, but a big fish. Great debate among the faithful raged for many years over the possibility or impossibility of such an achievement. Some argued that there are no fish big enough to accomplish the feat. On the other hand, certain species of whales do have mouths large enough to swallow a man. The only problem was that these whales were plant-eating creatures. Sermons were preached denouncing those who cast doubt on the veracity of scripture. Monographs were written, claiming that Jonah absolutely could have been, or absolutely could not have been, swallowed by a whale.

No doubt had Jonah known of these great debates in later time, he would not have cared much one way or the other. He had all he could do to concentrate on his own precarious situation.

He probably spent some time trying to understand why he was where he was instead of having been drowned. Apparently he reached some pretty definite conclusions on this score, because when he was deposited on shore (in a most uncerimonious fashion) and when he heard for the second time the command to go to Nineveh, there was no hesitation on his part. The Bible puts it succinctly: "So Jonah arose and went to Nineveh, according to the word of the Lord."

> Jonah began to go into the city, going a day's journey. And he cried, "Yet forty days, and Nineveh shall be overthrown!"

Try to put yourself in Jonah's shoes. You did not want to come on this preaching mission in the first place. You'd done your level best to get out of it, but running away hadn't worked and the next thing you know you're in Nineveh.

Nineveh, this cesspool of a city! Large, dirty, corrupt. Its streets filled with strange-looking faces, people speaking in strange-sounding dialects. It's a noisy, boisterous city. The loud voices and vulgar laughter are enough to make you cringe. You've heard all the stories about this place, you've been told by people in the know that someone like yourself just wouldn't feel at home here. "An interesting place to visit," they said, "if you want a few days of . . . of . . . 'excitement,' but you wouldn't want to live there."

Now you know what they were talking about. As you pass down the streets, you see houses that at one time may have been quite beautiful. But no more. Peeling paint, rotting shingles, litter and waste are everywhere.

You come to a section where depravity seems to scrawl its obscene signature on every doorway. You see street-walkers dressed in the cheap, flashy clothing of their trade. A drunk staggers past you and falls over in the ditch. You pass an open door and the nauseating smell of unwashed human bodies and cheap wine almost knocks you down. You hear angry shouts, curses, the sound of chairs being knocked over, and then the dull thud of blows being exchanged. Across the street young men lounge sullenly. They stare at you with such malice that you can feel your hair rise at the back of your neck. You walk on quickly.

Time to do what you have to do. You see a small, unkempt oasis of some grass, a few shrubs, some uncared-for roses, and a bench. It's a poor enough excuse for what was intended to be a park. But it will do.

You glance around; only a few people are in sight—an old man is walking his mangy dog, a few kids are pitching pennies against a wall, a woman is struggling home with a basket of groceries. You stand next to a tree and announce in a quavery voice, "In 40 days, Nineveh, because of her wickedness, will be destroyed."

The old man glances at you with rheumy eyes, his dog sniffs in your direction; then they both resume their walk. The woman with groceries is too busy balancing her burden to pay attention. Only one of the boys is moved to make a remark. "Hey, look at that creep over there," he says in your direction.

You turn away and continue your journey. What greets you is more of the same: more poverty, more filth, more indifference, more brutality. Your distaste at what you see turns to indignation. Why can't these people have at least some measure of self-respect? How can they live this way—worse than animals!

You deliver your message again. This time in a louder, more forceful voice. A few people pause to listen. You're encouraged to expand on your theme. You walk on again, more rapidly this time. Indignation rises within you. You stop to speak again. And as you speak, the words of doom become large and powerful. Now a small crowd forms; even some well-dressed people stop to listen.

The anger builds inside you, until it turns into hot rage. Now you are shouting your denunciations with savage satisfaction. You note with perverse pleasure the bewilderment on the people's upturned faces—faces ravaged by the wickedness of this evil, God-forsaken city. On you go, driven by the fire that burns inside, till at last, hoarse and exhausted, you stumble to an open field outside the city. And as the flame inside you subsides and sleep nears, the afterglow is unbelievably delicious. You had no idea it was going to be like this! What a fool you were to run away from such a destiny!

So it happened with Jonah.

> And the people of Nineveh believed God; they proclaimed a fast, and put on sackcloth, from the greatest of them to the least of them.
>
> When God saw what they did, how they turned from their evil way, God repented of the evil which he had said he would do to them; and he did not do it. But it displeased Jonah exceedingly, and he was angry. And he prayed to the Lord and said, "I pray thee, Lord, is not this what I said when I was yet in my country? That is why I made haste to flee to Tarshish; for I knew that thou art a gracious God and merciful, slow to anger, and abounding in steadfast love, and repentest of evil. Therefore now, O Lord, take my life from me, I beseech thee, for it is better for me to die than to live."
>
> Then Jonah went out of the city and sat to the east of the city, and made a booth for himself there. He sat under it in the shade, till he should see what would become of the city (Jonah 3:5, 3:10-4:3. 4:5).

Jonah had no expectation that his mission would succeed. He

could not believe it when he learned that his warning of doom and destruction had been heeded by the people of Nineveh. It's not easy for a person who thinks he is a failure to face the fact that he has succeeded.

But there was more to Jonah's reaction than this. The truth is he was eager for the fireworks to start. He had done his job, now it was the Almighty's turn to do his—to hurl the fire from heaven. What a spectacle—to see the city of sin go up in smoke. Jonah could hardly wait.

As decent, moral folk, it's perfectly normal for us to express our dismay at Jonah's vindictive streak. "Now, now, Jonah," we think, "Is this any way for a good Christian to behave?"

If Jonah could respond, he would likely do so by asking a few questions. Questions such as: "Haven't you ever secretly longed for something terrible to happen to the guy at work who's after your job?" "You parents, have you never, when boiling with anger, given your child a stern warning and then hoped he would defy you so you could whop him good and feel perfectly justified?" "Have you never wished that the speeding driver who just forced you off the road would plow headlong into the telephone pole ahead?" "Haven't you privately exulted when some celebrity whom you despise lands in jail or suffers serious misfortune?"

Enough questions, Jonah. We withdraw our objections to your behavior.

And yes, we too have established ourselves east of the city and have wished for the annihilation of what we find offensive to our eyes and noses and ears.

May God have mercy on our souls, and upon your soul, Jonah, and upon all those whose destruction we have longed for in the secret places of our hearts.

> And the Lord God appointed a plant, and made it come up over Jonah, that it might be a shade over his head, to save him from his discomfort. So Jonah was exceedingly glad because of the plant. But when dawn came up the next day, God appointed a worm which attacked the plant, so that it withered. When the sun rose, God appointed a sultry east wind, and the sun beat upon the head of Jonah so that he was faint; and he asked that he might die, and said, "It is better for me to die than to live." But God said to Jonah, "Do you do well to be angry for the plant?" And he said, "I do well to be angry, angry enough to die." And the Lord said, "You pity the plant, for which you did not labor, nor did you make it grow, which came into being in a night and perished in a night. And should I not pity Nineveh, that great city, in which there are more than a hundred and twenty thousand

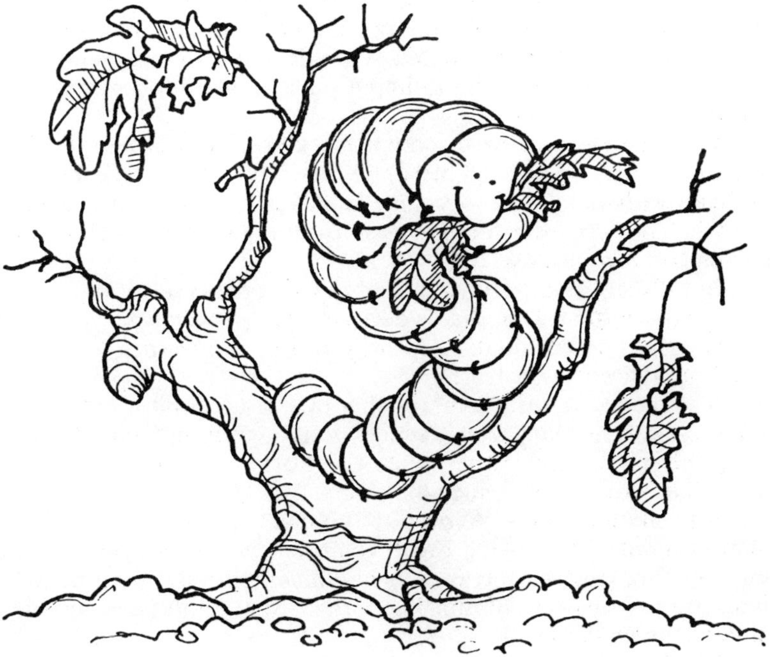

persons who do not know their right hand from their left, and also much cattle?'' (Jonah 4:6-11).

We've come at last to Jonah and the worm. Perhaps you have by this time forgotten all about the worm. Or have you begun to doubt that a worm was in the story at all?

Not only is a worm in the story, the worm is the *turning point* of the story, at least as far as Jonah is concerned. Of course, it is not hard to understand why people remember the whale and forget the worm when they think of Jonah. A whale swallowing a man is spectacular, incredible. A worm killing a plant is an all-too-common occurrence.

But the scripture reveals no partiality to either worm or whale. It says of the first: "And the Lord appointed a worm to attack the plant, so that it withered." The very same language is used in both passages, you see. Thus does the Almighty use from the greatest to the least to accomplish His purposes.

But if there is to be any hope at all for Jonah's salvation, it is the worm, not the great fish, that is decisive. Being swallowed was the big scare that prompted Jonah to do his job. But no one then or now has ever been redeemed by fear.

It is the worm on which Jonah's fate rests. (And it may be our fate as well.) The plant grows, shades Jonah, gives him relief from the heat, only to die and wither when the worm gets busy. And Jonah lapses into one of his predictable pouts.

And the Lord says, "You pity the plant, for which you did not labor, nor did you make it grow. It came and went overnight. Should I not pity Nineveh, that great city, in which there are more than 120 thousand persons who do not know their right hand from their left, and also much cattle?"

It's there the story ends, with a question mark. The story is not resolved. Does Jonah come to accept the truth—that the Lord is a "gracious God, merciful, slow to anger, and abounding in steadfast love?" Does that become a learning for him? Does he believe it and allow it to shape his life? Does he learn that God loves equally all creatures great and small, all men and women of every race and clan? Is he converted from the sins of indignation and self-righteousness to the way of kindness and compassion?

We do not know, for the story of Jonah ends with the Lord's sharp question hanging over Jonah's head. And the question remains, hanging sharply over our own heads.

Which is to say, of course, that the story does not end at all, but worms its way into our own human life story—yours and mine.

WHAT A KING WANTS . . .

The story of David and Bathsheba is a remarkable story, an incredible story. But not for the reason you think it is.

Most people, when they first read or hear the account of David's adultrous relationship with Bathsheba, find it hard to believe that the Bible is so explicit about such things. Not only does the book of II Samuel tell very bluntly what happened, it also reveals that David, the greatest of all the kings of Israel, indulged in the kind of immorality one simply does not expect from the composer of the beloved 23rd Psalm. Some people are scandalized by the story—scandalized, but still eager to hear every last detail of David's infamous behavior.

The first part of the story, naturally enough, makes for great Hollywood material. We can see the camera focusing on the handsome king as he walks in the cool of the evening on the rooftop of his house. He is all alone, seemingly deep in thought, when all at once he freezes, stands stock still. Now the camera follows the direction of his gaze and we see what has gripped his attention. It is a woman. Unaware that she is being watched, she is languidly bathing herself. No wonder David is stonestruck; the loveliness of her face and form are beyond words. She is exquisitely beautiful . . .

Cut. Enough of the Hollywood scenario. The scripture text does not embellish, does not dwell seductively on the scene. Nor does it suggest, as does the Hollywood version, that Bathsheba knew well enough what she was doing, that she was fully aware King David always took his rooftop walk at the same time every evening. No, Bathsheba is not to blame for what happens. This is especially noteworthy when we remember that, often enough in the pages of scripture, the woman *is* cast in the role of seductress.

There is no pre-meditation here—on anyone's part. The story begins with the words: "It happened." It simply happened, that's all. It happened that David saw Bathsheba, felt physical desire and acted on it. David was blameworthy in what happened, there can be no doubt of that, but there was no calculation ahead of time, no secret scheming.

There is this about temptation that sometimes deceives us—suddenly, without warning, it confronts. Given some time to think it over, to ponder the consequences, we likely would not succumb. But here it is in front of us—the chance to tell a half-truth, to utter the cutting remark, to cheat, to misrepresent—and before we know it, we have done the unthinkable. Small wonder that Jesus urged his followers to pray: "Lead us not into temptation."

David was tempted, and he sinned. He knew it was sin. And so do we. Any society that hopes to survive dare not condone adultery, any more than it can condone murder, theft, or perjury. If men are permitted to take other men's wives at will, if women are allowed to take other women's husbands whenever they wish, the fabric of that society has begun to unravel. Soon it will come apart at the seams. Trust and trustworthiness within the social contract are essential; without them, anarchy rises like a flood.

Whereas murder, adultery, theft, and perjury were once crimes of the dregs of society, today, with the possible exception of murder, these activities have all gone respectable. They are engaged in (with the proper touch of class, of course) by the high-placed, the influential, the celebrities among us. And the question arises—are adultery, theft, perjury, no longer "wrong"? I leave the question for you to answer—for yourself, for your children.

David was faced with no such question. He knew the Commandments; he knew the penalty for adultery. David's problem came at another point. He was, after all, the king. He enjoyed his kingly prerogatives. He had come to know the taste of "what I want is what I can get." And it is only a step from that point to: "What I can get is what I *mean to have*." It's the problem of power we're talking about now. Power begs to be used; it *insists* on being used. David saw Uriah's wife. He wanted her. He took her. Such are the uses of power.

And here might it have ended; a sin in secret, known only to God. The kind of sin you and I are familiar enough with, if we are honest. But, as we discover to our horror, sometimes the seeds of sin bear fruit. The scripture says simply: "And the woman conceived; and she sent and told David, 'I am with child.'"

No doubt the message did not concern the king overmuch. There was time; there were remedies . . . and he *was* the king. His command was law. All would be taken care of easily enough.

David's error in this is one we too commit. We suppose sin can be managed. After all, ours is a management society. Universities offer degrees in how to manage time, money, people, even institutions. Surely then a few indiscretions, a mere handful of problems, can be easily managed. All it takes is a little will power, a few discreet adjustments, and some common sense.

Let us see how David managed. The logical step, of course, was to get Bathsheba and her husband together and let nature take its course. No problem there. Uriah was on the front, fighting under the command of David's top general, Joab. As commander-in-chief, David issues a terse order by messenger to Joab: "Send me Uriah the Hittite." Uriah is sent. And the scripture says:

> When Uriah came to him, David asked how Joab was doing, and how the people fared, and how the war prospered (2 Samuel 11:7).

And so the deceit begins for David—the keeping up of appearances, the careful thought before each statement, the solicitous inquiries about Uriah's health and welfare. "How goes it, Uriah? Beastly hot, isn't it? The war is going well? Good, good! Sit back, Uriah, enjoy yourself."

There is something in David's nature that loathes the whole business. He is king! Yet here he is, behaving like a nervous fool, kowtowing to a common soldier. He cuts the interview short. "Well then, Uriah old sport, time for you to run along home, to your . . . " He cannot finish.

> And Uriah went out of the king's house, and there followed him a present from the king (2 Samuel 11:8).

"A present from the king," says the text. A guilt gift, Uriah, if you will open your eyes a bit. But that is not Uriah's nature. He is one of those blind, trusting fellows who prides himself above all else in his observance of the amenities and in faithful performance of duty. The law commanded soldiers to be celibate. Uriah would keep the law.

The king is frustrated, of course. So he tries a second time. The next night he has Uriah as his guest again, and this time breaks out the booze. And if the thought of David's play-acting pained us before, the performance this time is too unbearable to contemplate. But it does meet with the success David had hoped for. Uriah is sent off to his house starry-eyed drunk.

Again to no avail. Next morning David is told that Uriah has not gone home to his wife, but has slept in the king's servant quarters. Poor David. The whole business would have been so utterly laughable, were it happening to someone else.

And poor us when we find ourselves in similar straits. There are few things more frustrating than dealing with a saint. We confide a problem and instead of receiving a sympathetic nod, "That's too bad; I know what you're going through," we get instead a horrified stare of disbelief. Plagued by some guilt, we explain our situation to a friend. But rather than give us the absolution we had hoped for—"That's all right, I'd have done the same thing myself"—our friend says, "Boy, you *ought* to be feeling guilty."

Not only does Uriah frustrate David's plans, he doubles the king's guilt by his impeccable behavior and unswerving loyalty. In his anger, it is easy for David to think: "This fool deserves to die; he's brought it on himself." With a touch of malicious irony, the king has Uriah carry his own death warrant. It's an order to Joab. David probably didn't even seal it. He knew Uriah was too honest to read something not meant for his eyes. Curse his stupid honesty! The message reads: "Set Uriah in the forefront of the hardest fighting, and then draw back from him, that he may be struck down and die."

And so the plot extends—adultery, deception, murder. The death of Uriah *is* premeditated. This is no crime of passion, but a deed of coldblooded calculation. It is carried out by Joab without question. And the plot expands even more, to include an accomplice. The orders are given, the battle commences, and Uriah falls, fatally wounded—a victim to the last.

But the story does not end here. Joab sends word to the king that Uriah is dead. And David, fully confident that all will now be well, sends back a message to his general, which reveals how he is handling the death of his faithful soldier. The message states:

> Do not let this matter trouble you, for the sword devours now one and now another . . . (2 Samuel 11:25).

At first glance, this may appear to be a kind of dark comedy, the ultimate in royal sarcasm.

The truth is that David has already convinced himself that Uriah's death was simply a fortune of war. It is the timeless fatalism of the warrior. "If a rock, an arrow, a bullet has your name on it, why then, it's all over for you."

In the same way we seek to absolve ourselves of the consequences of wrongdoing. Carelessly, half deliberately, we break a confidence with a friend, and rather than admit to ourselves we have done wrong we say, "Well the story would have gotten out anyhow. I'm really not to blame." At school or at work, we decide to short-cut an assignment by taking credit for someone else's work. If the outcome is less than satisfactory, we tell ourselves that the teacher, the boss, has always had it in for us anyhow. "Besides, everyone else cheats, why shouldn't I?" We begin by deceiving others; in the end we deceive ourselves. So it was with David.

> When the wife of Uriah heard that Uriah her husband was dead, she made lamentation for her husband. And when the mourning was over, David sent and brought her to his house, and she became his wife, and bore him a son (2 Samuel 11:26-17).

And they all lived happily ever after? The story told—a king's will done, all perfectly legal and respectable. Kings and chiefs and emperors and presidents have been getting away with this kind of thing for centuries before and since David and Bathsheba. In the Near Eastern culture of David's time, a king's actions were above the law. If he wanted the property of one of his subjects, he simply took it. If he wanted someone's wife, he needed only to crook his finger. If he desired the death of a subject, he merely issued the command.

But not so in Israel, not among the people of God. No one stood above the law. The commandments of God applied equally to king and commoner.

I said at the outset that the story of David and Bathsheba is an incredible story. It is incredible because of what happened next, incredible that a ruling monarch should be held accountable for his wrongdoing.

For the text says,

> But the thing that David had done displeased the Lord (2 Samuel 11:27).

This is a simple sentence, but the implications of it are staggering. Nathan, a prophet of the Lord, is sent to King David. And he tells the king a story.

> There were two men in a certain city, the one rich and the other poor. The rich man had very many flocks and herds; but the poor man had nothing but one little ewe lamb, which he had bought. And he brought it up, and it grew up with him and with his children;

it used to eat of his morsel, and drink from his cup, and lie in his bosom and it was like a daughter to him. Now there came a traveler to the rich man, and he was unwilling to take one of his own flock or herd to prepare for the wayfarer who had come to him, but he took the poor man's lamb and prepared it for the man who had come to him (2 Samuel 12:1-4).

David, good king that he was, flared up in anger at such a miscarriage of justice. "As the Lord lives, the man who has done this deserves to die; and he shall restore the lamb fourfold, because he did this thing, and because he had no pity."

Then David broke off. Did the prophet really speak to him, or did he read the truth at last in Nathan's steadfast gaze?

"You are the man."

Should we pray God to spare us such terrible confrontation with the truth about ourselves? Such a prayer would be understandable, for the knowledge of such truth can devastate. But the sudden revelation of truth, painful as it is, may be the only thing that can save us. For once the lies, the deceptions, the cheating begin, they grow and grow until we lose our souls.

Let us pray rather for the truth from God. For his truth is born of love—for us, for all.

And David said, "I have sinned against the Lord." And in that admission was the beginning of his salvation. Only then could he begin to face himself again. Yes, he had to bear the consequence of his wrongdoing; that was painful. His son was taken from him. Confession never undoes the wrong. But it can restore us to right relationship with God, with those we have wronged, with ourselves. It can open the way to the love of God that takes the shape of life forgiven, restored—for a David, for a me, for a you.

THE WIDOW OF ZAREPHATH

A storyteller is only as good as his audience.
All it takes to reduce the best storyteller in the world to stammers and stutters is the presence of one thorough-going sceptic among his hearers. Imagine, for example, what it would be like trying to tell the story of "Goldilocks and the Three Bears" if one of your youthful listeners kept interrupting you.

"Once upon a time there were three bears, who lived together in a house of their own, in a wood."
"Bears don't *really* live in houses, do they?"
"Well, in this story they did."
"Were they real live bears?"
"Yes, of course,"
"I thought real live bears live in dens."
"Well, these bears lived in a *house!*"
"Oh."
"They had each a bowl for their porridge: a little bowl for the little wee bear; and a middle-sized bowl for the middle-sized bear; and a great big bowl for the great big bear."
"What's porridge?"
"It's some kind of soup or stew."
"Bears don't eat soup, do they?"
"These bears did."
"I thought bears eat berries and honey and things."
"Well, these bears ate porridge."
"Out of bowls?"
"Yes, out of bowls."
"I don't believe bears eat porridge or live in houses or any of this. Tell me a different story."

Do you see why I insist that a storyteller is only as good as his audience? When you put yourself in the hands of a storyteller, you've got to lay your skepticism to rest for a while. Stories are to sit back and enjoy, not to take apart like a crayfish that is dissected in biology class.

The kind of truth the storyteller is handling isn't measurable by inches or feet or mathematical equations or scientific formulas. No, he's dealing with truth of a different kind—truth about people and their goodness and badness, their nobility and depravity.

And in some cases, as in stories from the Bible, the truth of the stories may also have to do with God. Remember this point as we think about the story of the widow of Zarephath.

This story begins impressively: "The word of the Lord came to Elijah," a decidedly grander sound than "once upon a time." "The word of the Lord came to Elijah."

We could spend a lot of time on this character, Elijah, because he is definitely one of the VIP's of the Old Testament. Elijah was a notable prophet. His mission had been to tell King Ahab that the Lord had declared a moratorium on rain and snow and dew and every kind of wetness. That meant lots of nice, sunny weather, but it also meant drought. And drought meant no harvest. And no harvest meant famine.

So King Ahab was somewhat less than overjoyed at hearing the news Elijah the prophet brought him. When Elijah's predictions were seen to have been accurate, Ahab was anxious to get his hands on the prophet. So following the Lord's directions, Elijah decides to lay low for awhile.

We've already noted that Elijah was important; in the vernacular, he was a "somebody." And the people who are "somebodies," usually have the good judgment to know when to speak up and when to pipe down. A "somebody" who doesn't have that kind of perspicacity, who keeps speaking up all the time, usually doesn't last long as a "somebody." Especially if someone like Ahab is in charge of things.

At any rate Elijah listens when the Lord says, "Now hear this." And you will note that almost all the "somebodies" in the Bible had that much in common—when the Lord spoke, they paid attention. Nearly everybody else preferred not to be bothered, because the Lord had this irritating habit of expecting people to obey some laws, or stand up in public and preach, or make sacrifices. It was all very inconvenient. So, rather than pay attention, most folks just ignored the word of the Lord; until finally, they weren't able to hear Him at all.

At any rate, Elijah paid attention when the Lord said:

The Widow of Zarephath

> Arise, go to Zarephath, which belongs to Sidon, and dwell there. Behold I have commanded a widow to feed you. So he arose and went to Zarephath; and when he came to the gate of the city, behold, a widow was there gathering sticks (I Kings 17:8-10).

Zarephath was a city in Sidon. To get there Elijah has to leave his own country and go to foreign soil. As he approaches the gate to the city he sees a woman picking up the dead sticks from beneath the small shrubs of the barren earth, the source of the poor people's firewood.

Our story here contains an important contrast in the status of our two main characters. The first time we met Elijah, he was making a grand announcement to King Ahab about the word of the Lord. But in our first encounter with the widow of Zarephath, she's bending over, picking up sticks from the ground.

The reason for this contrast, of course, is that Elijah is a "somebody" and the widow isn't a "somebody." Like all the people in the Bible who aren't "somebodies," the widow is "just plain folks." Nothing derogatory is meant by that designation. After all, there's room for only so many "somebodies" in the world. They're either very smart or very rich or very powerful or very good or very bad. Or some combination of all those things.

But the widow of Zarephath? We're never even told what her name is. That's why we must keep referring to her as "the widow of Zarephath." She and you and I fit into the same category—"just plain folks."

And that's why her story is important. If she does anything worth remembering, we will sit up and pay attention. Not because she's gifted or famous. But precisely because she isn't; because she's one of us.

When Elijah sees her there, gathering sticks, he calls to her and says: "Bring me some water to drink."

This authoritarian demand by Elijah may cause us to react negatively toward the prophet. The least he could have done was to toss a "please" in there somewhere.

But remember that Elijah knew perfectly well that he was "somebody" and that the widow was "just plain folks." Wasn't she walking around in poor clothes gathering sticks? And wasn't he a prophet who had confronted King Ahab? Remember also that all this happened in those former days when a woman "knew her place." It was woman's duty to wait upon the orders of a man. So we should not judge Elijah harshly. Besides, he was very thirsty.

And as the widow turns to do his bidding, Elijah remembers that besides being very thirsty, he is also very hungry. So he adds, "And

while you're at it, bring me some bread also."

If criticism is due Elijah, this is the place. He stands guilty of that breach of human decency we might call the "oh by the way" offense. Surely you have experienced this offense yourself.

It's what happens when your husband is enumerating the expenses of the things you've asked him to buy at the store and then says in his best off-hand manner: "Oh, by the way, I picked up a new set of golf clubs—a real bargain—only ninety-five dollars."

It's what happens when your wife asks you to fix the clothesline in the back yard and then adds, "Oh, by the way, while you're out there, how about trimming the hedge, cleaning out the rain gutters, changing the tires on my car, and painting the shutters?"

Or it's what happens when a friend from church calls you to ask how your garden is doing and then says, "Oh, by the way, how about serving as head of the finance committee for the next seven years?"

We have a right to be upset when that happens to us. It shows a low regard for our intelligence and our personhood. And a "somebody" like Elijah can be guilty of it the same as you or I.

But when he gives the widow this, "Oh, by the way, bring some bread too," she has an answer that jolts him. It jolts us as well. And from this point on, the story wears a dark, sober aspect.

The widow says,

> As the Lord your God lives, I have nothing baked, only a handful of meal in a jar, and a little oil in a cruse; and now, I am gathering a couple of sticks, that I may go in and prepare it for myself and my son, that we may eat it, and die (I Kings 17:12).

What revealing words they are. Suddenly we see the widow of Zarephath in a new light. "Just plain folks" she may be, but she is also a woman of incredible courage and dignity. There is a severe famine in the land. But she will not lie down in despair. She will not rail futilely against the gods. No, she will do what she knows must be done. And then, having done all that can be done, she and her son will die, but with their dignity intact.

Hearing these words, Elijah finally sees the honest dignity of this woman. And he responds with two of the most comforting words the human ear can hear:

"Fear not."

Those words echo through scripture. In Isaiah the Lord God says to His people:

> Fear not: for I have redeemed thee, I have called thee by thy name; thou art mine (Isaiah 43:1).

We remember too the angel's message to the shepherds:

> Fear not, for behold I bring you good tidings of great joy (Luke 2:10).

And we recall the blessed words of Jesus:

> Fear not, little flock, for it is your Father's good pleasure to give you the kingdom. (Luke 12:32).

How we need to hear those words of assurance. "Fear not." "Don't be afraid." They must come from someone we respect, someone we trust. Only a "mommy" or a "daddy" can say them to a youngster who wakes in terror from a nightmare. Only a heavenly Father can comfort us with his own "Fear not" in the face of the terrors of our existence—pain, separation, death.

What did those words mean to the widow of Zarephath, we may wonder. Did she hear them as an expression of sympathy, as a polite gesture? Or did the words of Elijah carry the assurance he intended?

We cannot know. But we do know that Elijah instructed her to do as she had planned, to use the last of the meal and the oil but also to make him some bread. And then he told her:

> For thus says the Lord the God of Israel. "The jar of meal shall not be spent, and the cruse of oil shall not fail, until the day that the Lord God sends rain upon the earth" (I Kings 17:14-15).

And then the text says, "She went and did as Elijah said."

It may be argued that she had nothing to lose. She and her son faced death anyhow, so it showed no great faith to do what the prophet told her. But there is more to it than that. Either a woman is a woman of faith or she is not. Either a man is a man of faith or he is not. Faith is a long-time process. It's not something you suddenly "get" when there's nothing to lose anymore.

The widow of Zarephath had great courage and great dignity. That much we already knew. And now we learn she had great faith as well.

She could have said, "I've got to keep what little I have for myself. Go on to the next house, if you want something to eat. Go to the wealthy section of town. I can't give you anything."

She could have said that and we would not have blamed her. We've said it ourselves often enough, God knows.

And God knows too that the blessing cannot be given without the commitment. That's the way it has always been. The promise to the widow that the meal would never run out could not take effect until she had scraped out the last bit, turned it upside down and pounded on the bottom for meal enough to bake one last loaf.

Our commitment comes first—then follows the blessing, and always a greater blessing than we had expected or dared to hope for.

God knows one other thing too. It's a thing we have such a hard time learning. The widow learned it. Elijah probably learned it too. It is that we are never asked to give more than we can give. We may be asked to give much, maybe even a great deal, maybe a lot more than we feel is convenient. But never more than we *can* give.

If we do not acknowledge that truth, or if we are unwilling to act on it, our refusal is a foolish and maybe even a sinful thing. And we have explored the story of the Widow of Zarephath and have not heard the word of the Lord.

THE SEARCH FOR HOME

Occasionally in the biblical narrative, we run across people who do not figure prominently in the history of God's people. They are casually noted by name, or in some cases are described as contributing to an interesting episode in the life of one of the Bible's central characters. Such a person is the man, Barzillai the Gileadite, whose story is told in 2 Samuel 19.

Barzillai had done a great service for King David at a time when the king was in danger of defeat by his enemies. But now the crisis has passed and David is returning in triumph to his home in Jerusalem. As a reward to Barzillai, the king offers to take him along to Jerusalem and look after him the rest of his days.

Now most of us would have jumped at such a chance. But Barzillai does not. He asks David if he might be permitted to return to his home, and since he is an old man, he says it this way:

> Pray, let your servant return, that I may die in my own city, near the grave of my father and my mother (2 Samuel 19:37).

His request is granted, and Barzillai makes his exit from the pages of scripture.

We have to wonder about Barzillai and his strong feeling for his home—home as the place where he could spend the rest of his days and be buried with his parents. Was Barzillai afraid to leave home, or was he genuinely attached to that piece of land he called his own? I suspect it was the latter. In a way that very few of us can feel perhaps, Barzillai, as have many others in the far past and even the more recent

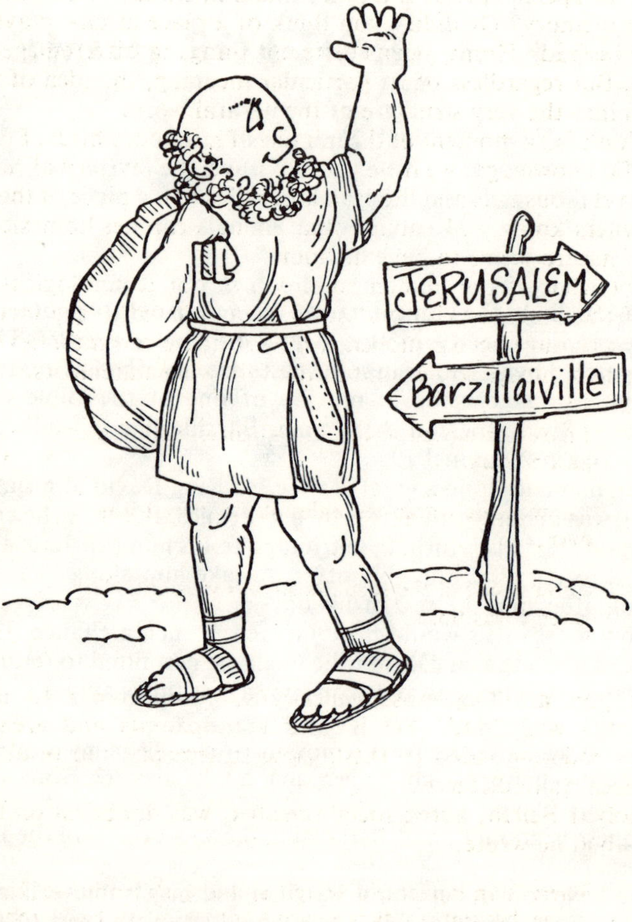
JERUSALEM
Barzillaiville

past, felt a sacred attachment to the place he called home. He had been born there, had lived there all his life, knew it intimately and prized it above any privileges and honors he might win at the royal court.

What about your understanding of home? When you see the word *home,* what flashes into your mind? Is it a piece of land? Is it a house, an apartment? Is it a place that still stands or one that exists only in memory? Or didn't you think of a place at all—maybe some people instead? Home means different things to different people, of course. But regardless of its particular meaning, the idea of home is written into the very structure of the natural world.

Think for a moment of the miracle of migratory birds. For all our scientific knowledge, we have yet to unravel the mystery of how birds can travel thousands and thousands of miles to the place of their birth. Pet owners know well enough that animals can get homesick. Each part of nature seems to have its home.

But what of the human condition in our technological age? Is part of the problem with our world today related to the fact that so many of us have been removed from our home communities?

Take a minute to respond to the following statements.

I have not moved, changed residences, within the past 5 years.	Yes	No
I now reside within ten miles of the place I was born.	Yes	No
I now reside at the same location my parents did when I was born.	Yes	No

If you are like most Americans, your answer to all three statements was "no." Yet if your grandparents and great-grandparents had responded to these same statements, the results would have been quite different.

Robert Bellah, noted social scientist, was doubtless on the right track when he wrote:

> There is an immense nostalgia and longing for home, for being at home, but our reality is an acute homelessness. Every religion must deal with the problem of home and homelessness, must develop its resources of symbol and myth in this area.
> (In *The Christian Century,* February 14, 1973, p. 206).

All of this has implications for us as women and men of faith. There was a time when Christians were urged to transcend any feelings of homelessness they had by looking forward to a "heavenly home." The harder life was and the less they felt "at home" in this world, the more appealing the after-life appeared, as in the spirituals:

> Deep river, my home is over Jordan.

and

> Swing low, sweet chariot
> Comin' for to carry me home.

As a boy, I can recall listening to the radio and hearing a then-popular gospel song:

> This world is not my home,
> I'm just a passin' through.
> My treasure is laid up
> Somewhere beyond the blue.
> The angels beckon me
> From heaven's open door.
> And I can't feel at home
> In this world any more.

There are not many of us willing to settle for that anymore. We have gone beyond that imagery of heaven as a home "somewhere beyond the blue." That was bad faith anyhow, to be so intent on the life to come that we ignore the only life we know intimately now—the present life.

Robert Bellah is right that we need to develop resources of symbol and myth about home in our religion. We need to do so in a time when home as a place, as a location, has all but disappeared, and in a time when home as an institution is threatened by an ever-rising tide of broken marriages. The roots of our faith offer us some guidance.

The Bible makes clear, not only in the story of Barzillai, but in other places as well, that home as a location, a geographical space, *is* important. Yet, for most of us, the place of our birth and growing-up years is gone—leveled by the bulldozer of "progress" or standing in alien stubbornness, surrounded by proud new houses. That being the case, it is vital that the places in which we reside today—be they modern split-levels or cramped apartments—speak to us truly as home, a place where we can retreat for refreshment and rest and renewal. These places where we live should have a "homey" atmosphere. They should say to us, and to any who visit, "This is the place where *we* live; this is unmistakably *our* home."

We need not try to outdo the neighbors by having the most luxurious lawn or the fanciest fireplace. An atmosphere which says "home" to you and me does not depend on the numbers of dollars we spend on a house and furnishings.

But the place where we live *is* important. It should help identify who we are. I like to go into homes where the youngsters' drawings are displayed at a prominent place, where the hobbies and interests of the family are immediately visible. That says something to me about that home. Often we apologize when a visitor stops by and the house looks lived in. We get defensive and say, "Oh, this place is a mess!" But why should we say it's a mess unless the mess reflects the fact that our family itself is a mess?

We should prefer neatness to sloppiness. But sometimes I think we overdo the neatness routine. I think each person in the family should have a place in the home exclusively his or hers. Privacy is important in a world where we are constantly imposed upon by others. Maybe parents should find better ways of teaching their children to be responsible than by insisting their rooms always be neat and clean. There is something precious in the privilege of having a room where you can open the door and say, "This place may look like a disaster area; but it's *my* disaster area, and I *like* it here."

One more word about home as a place. In addition to private spaces that say "home" to us, we need public places that do the same. As I think about the geographical area I live in, I find it depressing to realize there are all too few public places that are important to me. Somehow the parking lot of a huge shopping center just doesn't do it. With buildings occupying more and more land, communities need to provide spaces designed just for relaxation and recreation. Such places should feature grass, not asphalt; trees, not steel and concrete.

We have noted that a place to call home is important and our faith supports such a claim. But the Judeo-Christian heritage also teaches, unmistakably, that location is of secondary importance. What is essential for home is a certain kind of relationship.

This truth is perhaps best revealed in the gospel of Luke, where Jesus compares his lot with the creatures in nature and then declares that he can call no place his home.

> Foxes have holes, and birds of the air have nests;
> but the Son of man has nowhere to lay his head (Luke 9:58).

No doubt our Lord felt this lack keenly. So the feeling of homelessness we experience in our time is one our Lord shared while he was here on earth. For him, home had a special meaning. Once, when his mother and brothers came to see him, Jesus commented to the one who informed him of their presence, "Who is my brother, and sister, and mother" (Matthew 12:48-50).

Our first reaction to these words is to think how unfeeling Jesus appears to be about his own family. What we miss is his beautiful point about the importance of relationships. His disciples were those who had shared with him in the joys and troubles and just plain routine of everyday life. Holding them together was their commitment to each other and to the God they worshipped. Out of that relationship was born something solid and vital. It is not untrue to Jesus' words to say that for him, his "home" was there—in the company of the disciples.

When you stop to think about it, home is, above all else, the people who are there—people who accept you, with all your flaws and frayed ends and rough edges. Home is really home when you can go there and know they'll be glad to see you.

It's fine to quote Edgar Guest who wrote, "It takes a heap of livin' to make a house a home," if you realize that a home doesn't just happen by people living together. It takes effort on everyone's part—to be kind, to be honest, to be loving, to be responsible. Home, our Lord teaches us, is not the place, but the people—people committed to each other through good times and bad times. The search for home ends when we find people to whom we are committed—we to them, they to us.

Robert Frost wrote a poem in which a husband and wife, living on a New England farm, came home to discover a former hired hand at their house. Obviously exhausted and ill, the old hired man is given a meal. Leaving him to get some rest, Mary and Warren discuss what to do about their guest. They recall that the hired man has an older brother who lives just a few miles down the road.

> "His brother's rich—
> A somebody—director in the bank."
>
> "I think his brother ought to help."

They soon realize that the hired man did not go to his brother's place because he would not have felt welcome there. Instead, he had found his way to this farm because in some way he regarded it as home. And Mary says,

> "Warren, he has come home to die."

"Home?"

"Yes, what else but home? It all depends on what you mean by home."

"Home is the place where, when you have to go there, they have to take you in."

Maybe that is what Barzillai knew deep within himself when he rejected King David's generous offer. No royal gift could ever replace the meaning of "home."

In our search for home, we too may discover the importance of both place and relationships. And so, by God's grace, we will find the peace of our true home.

II.

And the story continues ...

YEAST, SALT AND SECRET AGENTS

I'm a sucker for spy stories. And judging from the great number of books, movies and tv shows which feature tales of espionage and secret agents I'm not alone in my predilection. People have always been fascinated by tales of underground activity, of cloaks and daggers, of secret messages and deadly nighttime visitors whose calling cards are cement blocks tied to eternally silenced victims.

Maybe it's that simple. I, along with almost everyone else, enjoy a good scare once in a while, even if I must get it vicariously by hearing a story. Still, there's more to spy stories than scares and thrills. There's also the element of travel in strange countries, exciting cities: London, Berlin, Moscow, Paris. I've never yet read a book about espionage transpiring in the exotic cafes of Tinkerville, Ohio.

It is the element of the unexpected—of life lived on the knife's edge—which is a spy story's most distinctive feature. At any moment, the best laid plans, the most secret of communications might be uncovered. But also, at any moment, the desperate mission might meet with overwhelming success. Because life is precariously balanced in this way, every simple pleasure takes on great significance. A walk down the dark corridor is not commonplace, it's a drama. The daytime colors and sounds in the park are intensified. The spy, in our literary tradition, has a zest for life, a keen awareness of its tastes and smells that are heightened by watchfulness.

Then finally, there is the exhilaration one always gets in knowing one is on the right side doing battle against the forces of evil. The enemy is cold-blooded, murderous, absolutely without moral principle. Thus, capture or death for the cause of right seems as noble as it does tragic.

One of Jesus' parables relates to this subject of spies and espionage. The story is in Matthew:

> Jesus told them another parable: "The Kingdom of heaven is like yeast. A woman takes it and mixes it with a bushel of flour, until the whole batch of dough rises" (Matthew 13:33, Today's English Version).

We may think first of the finished product—the loaves of bread. What was Jesus trying to say about God's kingdom—in what way is it like bread? We recall how Christ fed the multitude with the bread and fishes and also how he broke bread and gave it to his disciples seated with him for a last meal.

But this little story about the woman and her baking invites a broader implication. It would have been helpful if Jesus had expanded on his parable, perhaps interpreted it for his listeners. The parable immediately preceding this one is that of the mustard seed—the tiny seed which after planting grows up to be a very large shrub. Now the mustard seed in that story seems comparable to the yeast the woman hid in the loaves. It took only a tiny bit of yeast to do the job of making the dough rise. What did Jesus mean when he said God's rule is comparable to yeast in the dough? Maybe he meant that the kingdom of God is hardly noticeable to the human view but that its aftereffects are quite significant.

There is another enlightening reference to yeast in the New Testament. Writing to his Christian friends at Corinth, Paul noted that they were having trouble dealing with one of their number whose personal morality was not the highest quality. Paul warned them they had to deal with the situation before it became destructive to the whole congregation. "Don't you know," he said, "that just a small bit of yeast leavens the whole loaf?"

We can infer from these references that the Christian's life might be symbolized by the yeast. Hardly noticeable outwardly, it is really a significant force for good in the world, much as in the proverb about a tiny candle being enough to confound the darkness. Jesus once said to his disciples: "You are the light of the world" (Matthew 5:14). He also told them they were the salt of the earth: salt, the substance that adds zest and seasoning. It's amazing how the addition of salt to food changes its whole character, just as yeast changes bread.

Now the presence of Christians in the world—as light or salt or yeast—is not to be a spectacular affair. In fact, Christians will likely be hidden from the common view, just as by looking at a lump of dough before it has risen you cannot tell whether or not the yeast is present.

The committed Christian is a member of a minority group that's working within the larger society toward the end that God's kingdom will come. The Christian way is at odds with the generally accepted ideas of society. An important theme in church literature has been the image of the Christian as an alien, a stranger in an unfriendly world. It requires no great imagination to use the modern phrase, "secret agent," as still another image to describe the Christian calling.

The more I think about it, the more appropriate the comparison between the Christian and the secret agent seems. Maybe the first parallel lies in the recruitment of both. As Soren Kierkegaard said:

> I am, as it were, a spy in the service of the highest. The police also use spies. They do not always pick out men whose lives have been the purest and best, quite the contrary: they are cunning, crafty offenders. . . .
> Alas, thus does God use sinners.

That should be a sober reminder that God never chooses people to be his agents because of their flawless characters.

What are some other comparisons between the spy and the Christian? The secret agent always knows only a small part of the whole intelligence game. For all he or she knows, that person in the phone booth across the room may also be working as a fellow agent. The spy is never in on top level decisions, nor is the spy called upon to achieve great success. The job is to carry out assignments with as much skill as possible.

Just so, the Christian is never asked to devise a plan to save the world. That has been taken care of by the home office. The Christian's job is to be faithful to his or her Lord, no matter what. Then too the Christian may be surprised at finding others doing the work of heaven in most unlikely places. No less than for a spy, life for the Christian is filled with the unexpected. And who can yet judge what is success or failure in God's eyes? Paul Scherer asks: "How many of us are capable of leaving what we have been accustomed to call our liabilities where they belong—to the future and to God? You don't know yet—and you can't know—where to enter any of them in the ledger: credit side or debit."

Back to the spy's duties. The spy is called on to move into dangerous territory, perhaps to take assignment in a country where the philosophy of government is quite different and where freedom of the individual is not recognized. Thus the secret agent may be at odds with the thinking of the people. The spy must move within their social circles, eat in the same restaurants, yet maintain a loyalty to a different way of life.

The Christian also lives in a society which has a set of values different from his or her own. The Christian values people more than things, love more than power. The person of faith knows that the world at large operates on the principle of looking out for number one. Sometimes the Christian also falls into that pattern, but the eyes are on a higher principle: "Seek first the kingdom of God." In fact, the Christian's style of life is patterned, not after the people one encounters, but after the words and example of Jesus Christ.

Now it's true that spy stories are full of suspense and drama, because that's what makes for entertainment. However, I've read that espionage work is not in reality all that exciting. There's a great deal of routine involved—reams of paper work, much sitting around waiting for something to happen. Whenever I imagine the life of a spy, I see a person sitting in one of those passenger compartments on the train from Dresden to Prague, getting ready to pass on to another agent the microfilm that will save the free world. But perhaps I've seen too many movies—spies probably don't even ride trains anymore.

It is no secret that the life of a Christian isn't exactly glamorous. Like anyone else, the Christian may spend most of his or her time just fulfilling the day-to-day obligations and jobs that have to be done. Moments of exhilaration and inspiration are rather rare.

Naturally, we can carry the analogy only so far. There are some obvious differences between the spy and the Christian. Especially is this true of the methods used. To a spy the ends justify the means; whatever activities are required to get the job done, one engages in, and that can mean lying, stealing, even killing. The Christian on the other hand, knows that if his or her actions are not loving, nor consistent with the goal of God's kingdom, then all is lost.

Another difference relates to attitude. While the spy may despise the enemy (and this hatred may even help in doing the job better), Christians are called on to love even those who would do them harm. The Christian knows that God's call to be his secret agent is for the very purpose of saving the people most opposed to him.

Some may find the very comparison between spies and Christians a bit too farfetched. Yet I recall how Jesus sent out his disciples two by two and told them: "I send you out as sheep in the midst of wolves; so be wise as serpents and innocent as doves" (Matthew 10:16). What better instructions could there be for secret agents? I recall too that in the early days of the church, Christianity was forced to become an underground movement, that Paul had to flee many times for his life because the authorities came to arrest him. Finally, I remember that the work of the first Christians was so subversive to the status quo that their enemies ruefully acknowledged that the followers of Christ were turning the world upside down.

Most of us don't find it very appealing to be the yeast in the dough, the salt in the stew, the spy out in the cold. Yet that is our calling: to be God's humble, loving secret agents in a world that needs and waits for his kingdom to come.

WHO MADE ME A JUDGE OVER YOU?

Some of the most serious and solemn things in life are only a twinkle of an eye away from being truly hilarious. Take, for example, a stranger-than-fiction event reported in the news some time ago.

The story told of a man who died a most untimely death. Or perhaps the opposite is true: the timing was so perfect that its occurrence brought him the national recognition denied him during his lifetime. This man died right in the middle of a wedding service. Now, of course, people have been known to die during weddings before. But this fellow was not a guest at the wedding. He was the groom.

No doubt it was a tragic, extremely upsetting event. What an ironic twist—to have tears of joy transformed into tears of shock and grief. A sad, sad tale without a doubt.

Why was it, then, that as I read this story in the newspaper, I began to feel a perverse tickle at my funnybone? First, I started to smile. Then I read further and began to snicker. And finally, in spite of my conscience which kept repeating, "But this is a sad, sad tale," I let out a whoop of laughter capable of rattling the coffee cups on our kitchen shelf.

Heaven help me, but it was *funny*. Especially when we learn that the whole thing ended up in court with the wife, or the prospective wife, claiming that they had indeed been married and that therefore her husband's, or her would-be husband's estate belonged to her. The dead man's parents were also there in court, arguing that the marriage had *not* taken place and that the woman had no rights to the property at all . . . the scheming little golddigger!

To be sure, all elements of comedy are there; farcical comedy guaranteed to delight any theatergoer. And all the stock characters are in the story, as well: the eligible bachelor tied to Mama's apron strings who finally gets lured to the altar; the bride who has used every trick in the book to get him there—laughing at his terrible jokes, telling him how handsome he is, what a brilliant thinker he is; the groom's parents who oppose the marriage because they see what the woman is after.

But finally, there he stands at the front of the church. The vows are taken; the groom reaches into his pocket for the ring. Suddenly he gasps and clutches at his chest. The minister sees what is happening so he starts reading the service as fast as he can and finally gets to the part . . . "and I now pronounce you husband and wife," just in the nick of time. At least that's what he tells the judge when the case comes to court.

Think of all the funny stories you've heard about contested wills, about families fighting over who will get Aunt Susie's antique music box, about the old man who wills all his possessions to his pet cat, about the umpteen last wills and testaments of one Howard Robard Hughes.

I believe the laughter that comes out of these stories is one of the healthiest of human reactions. The humor comes from the picture of men and women so wrapped up in trying to get something for themselves that they cannot see the foolishness, the utter stupidity of their actions. More than one family has been torn apart as brothers and sisters quarreled over their departed parents' possessions. What do the winners of such arguments achieve? A few pieces of cloth or pottery or wood which they take home and store away in a closet—there to remain till *they* die and *their* children quarrel over who will get what.

Greed, more than any other human frailty, is the producer of fools—young fools, old fools, and, in the biblical sense, damned fools.

That's what a question Jesus asked one day was all about.

A man came to Jesus and said: "Master, tell my brother to divide the family property with me."

We do not know the details of this dispute. Jewish law contained specific provisions on the matter of inheritance. But the man's request to Jesus was not unusual. Very often rabbis were asked to give authoritative answers to matters that were both religious and legal in nature.

Imagine the man's surprise, therefore, when Jesus asks him: "Man, who made me a judge or a divider over you?" Jesus isn't interested in the facts of the case; he sees something far more important.

He sees the foolishness, the pathetic foolishness, of two men, worshippers of the same God, sons of the same mother and father, separated from each other over the possession of a bit of property. He sees that the man has come to him with entirely the wrong question. The man should be asking about how he and his brother can be reconciled. Instead of that, he wants to use Jesus to help him get material things which have no lasting value.

How can this man and the people who are gathered around them come to see how ridiculous this quarrel really is? Jesus decides to tell a story. I have a feeling that, had the account of the man dying at his own wedding been in the news at that time, our Lord might have told that story. Instead he tells of a rich man, and he prefaces the parable with a word of warning.

> Be on your guard against greed of every kind, for even when a man has more than enough, his wealth does not give him life (Luke 12:15 NEB).

Or as another translation has it:

> A man's life does not consist in the abundance of his possessions (RSV).

How familiar those words are to us, and yet how hard it is to live them. Maybe Jesus knew that such words alone would not have the impact of a true-to-life story. Maybe that is why he told a humorous tale to illustrate his point.

Yes, a *humorous* tale. For this familiar parable is about a man who was, above all else, a fool. One of the best ways to grasp the humor of the story is to read it as Clarence Jordan paraphrased it.

> A certain rich fellow's farm produced well. And he held a meeting with himself and he said, "What shall I do? I don't have room enough to store my crops." Then he said, "Here's what I'll do: I'll tear down my old barns and build some bigger ones in which I'll store all my wheat and produce. And I will say to myself, 'Self, you've got enough stuff stashed away to do you a long time. Recline, dine, wine, and shine!'" But God said to him, "You nitwit, at this very moment your goods are putting the screws on your soul. All these things you've grubbed for, to whom shall they really belong?" That's the way it is with a man who piles up stuff for himself without giving God a thought.
> *(The Cotton Patch Version of Luke,* by Clarence Jordan, The Association Press, New York.)

Normally when we hear or read this parable, we think to ourselves: "What an evil person that rich man was; he got his just deserts." Every sermon I've heard and every commentary I've read takes this approach—the rich man did a wicked thing and God punished him for it.

But what is wicked about the rich man's actions? The harvest is larger than he had expected, so he builds bigger barns. Is that wicked? It sounds more like good business practice. Then he sits back and decides to enjoy himself for a while. Is that wicked? If it is, every one of us is in big trouble.

Call the rich man self-indulgent, if you will. That assessment has some truth in it. But surely it is stretching the point to argue that the rich man was guilty of committing great wickedness.

Furthermore, God does not punish the rich man in the parable. What kind of God would it be who strikes people dead because he doesn't like to see them enjoying the fruit of their labors? In the story God says to the man: "You fool." He does not say: "You wicked, wicked man," or "You terrible sinner," but "You nitwit! You fool!"

And he says, "This very night you must surrender your life; you have made your money— who will get it now?"

At last the point of the story hits home. The rich man had thought he was being so very clever—using his funds shrewdly, knowing just how and when to reinvest his capital. Hadn't it paid off? Wasn't he set for life? But in the end he discovered he was just fooling himself. He had spent his life in pursuit of material goods; what was there to show for it? Nothing. His hard-earned treasures must be left behind.

He is a fool, a laughable, pitiful fool.

The Psalmist was right when he wrote:

> Do not envy a man when he grows rich . . .
>   for he will take nothing when he dies,
>   and his wealth will not go with him (Psalm 49:16-17 NEB).

And Jesus says, "So is he who lays up treasure for himself and is not rich toward God."

Where do we fit into this picture?

Perhaps at two places. First, in the story of the rich man. Of course, there are some significant differences between him and us. We are not as wealthy as he; most of us are not at the point where we could sit back and relax into retirement, as he planned to do.

But in some ways we are the same. Like him, we often define people by their possessions. We use the expression: "How much is so and so worth?" and we mean by that phrase the measurement of a person's wealth in dollars and cents. But is that all we mean? How much *is* a man or a woman or a child worth? Is it not utter foolishness to speak in terms of dollars and cents? Yet we do it all the time.

We define ourselves by our possessions, especially in relationship to the possessions of others. You see the new car your friend has purchased. It is shiny and new and guaranteed to produce envy. And suddenly your own two-year-old model seems dirty and old, a poor thing indeed. Without knowing why, you feel depressed. Your sense of self-worth drops twenty points or so. The problem may be that you have foolishly defined yourself by your possessions, and you don't like the definition.

The reason this happens is the attention we give to the hucksters who tell us to buy things that will make us the envy of our friends. Or we're feeling low and someone tells us: "Go out and buy something; that's what I do whenever I get depressed." And it does seem indeed that buying, accumulating things, is the American hope of salvation, as evidenced by the huge crowds of people who jam the shopping centers in search of fellowship, entertainment, adventure and meaning.

Popular economic theories seem to validate this salvation-through-buying doctrine. For instance, the standard answer to a sluggish economy is: give everybody a tax break and then tell them to go out and spend like crazy. That philosophy doesn't ring true. Not only is it a simplistic answer, it also seems immoral—in light of the millions of people in our world literally dying for lack of food and shelter and health care.

But we are all conditioned by our surroundings. We know the nearly overwhelming compulsion that comes over us when we walk into the store and see that attractive whatever-it-is sitting so seductively on the counter. Elsie Boulding suggests a fresh understanding of this problem as she writes of being reared by her mother to be a "consumer queen." We can see what we are tempted to become when we witness a young lady on a tv news program rhapsodizing about Bloomingdale's department store and cheerfully admitting she had to move back to New York City because she is "hooked on Bloomys."

Then we see that Jesus' story about the rich man who defined his life by his possessions is a portrait of what we could very easily be ourselves. That's where I fit into the picture—and so do you.

There is one other place we fit into the picture, in the person of the man who came to Jesus and asked him to get him his share of the inheritance. Our spoken and unspoken prayers are much the same as that request. We're seldom so crass as to pray, "Lord, please make sure that the stock in which I invested climbs several points." We wouldn't want to offend by being so blatant. Only children who pray for a new bicycle are that crude—and that honest!

Instead we pray for things like happiness and success for ourselves and our families. But if we were pushed to define what we mean by happiness or success, we might discover that our prayers are in essence no different from that of the youngster who wants a bike.

Jesus told his disciples to pray for daily bread—that is, for the basic resources of life. God *is* the ultimate provider of our needs. But he is not the jolly Santa Claus, dispenser of unlimited goodies, that we would like him to be.

When Jesus asked, "Who made me a judge or a divider over you?" he was raising a basic question of faith. He was asking why we cannot see the foolishness of our love affair with material possessions.

Can we hear that question he asks—really hear it? Can we let it be for us a call to understand what in life is genuine, meaningful and lasting?

If we cannot, our foolishness may be beyond saving. We may be condemned fools. God forbid that it be so.

JUST AS WE ARE

It was a seminar—a seminar with the admirable theme: "Peacemaking." And it brought together speakers and participants from the historic "peace churches"—Mennonites, Friends, Brethren. In a group like that, the sight of a Bible should not have been a surprise to me.

And yet, as we stood up to stretch for a ten minute break, I found myself staring in disbelief, in horror, at a Bible lying open upon the table next to me. The cause of my shocked reaction lay in the appearance of the pages. From top to bottom, they were marked with underlinings and notations in ink of three or four shades of blue, with some red, yellow, and green thrown in for good measure.

For most observers that sight would have meant little more than that the owner of the volume was obviously a serious student of the scriptures. For me, however, those pages of underlinings aroused negative feelings buried in near-forgotten memories of childhood. For once, long ago, I had been warned by a finger-pointing adult that I must never, never, never put a pencil mark on the pages of my Bible. It was a well-meaning but overzealous Sunday School teacher who had uttered that "thou shalt not." I dimly recall the reason given for the ban was that the Bible was a holy book, and thus its pages should be kept pure, spotless, and unsullied by the pencil scratchings of such mere mortals as us children.

I've long ago discarded the superstitious notion that underlined pages of holy writ will doom its owner to perdition. After my initial shock at seeing that prolifically marked Bible on the table, I too admired that person's obvious devotion to its teachings. After all, I am a rational person, reasonably intelligent, mature enough to recognize the limitations of my childhood understandings of things.

If you believe what I just wrote, then please explain to me why in the Bibles that I own and use in my study there is nowhere to be found an underline or a note in the margin!

In the vocabulary of transactional analysis, my parent tape is being played with the volume turned up. In ordinary terms, what we're dealing with here is guilt.

Guilt feelings are part of human life. If my guilt feelings subconsciously will not allow me to write in Bibles, someone else's may prevent that person from stepping on cracks on the sidewalk or some other equally irrational thing. Guilt is rooted in the earliest experiences of our lives. It is part of the mechanism that makes possible a sense of right and wrong, without which human society could not exist. So, although guilt may lead us into some rather unusual behavior patterns, it does have its uses. To illustrate this truth, we need only to be reminded of newspaper accounts about confessed killers who have no remorse, no guilt at all, for the brutal crimes they've committed. A person without a conscience, without the capacity to feel guilty, is not a fully developed human being.

As a relatively new parent, I am experiencing that which all parents go through in the effort to teach their offspring right from wrong. For, although none of us believe guilt is a good thing in and of itself, we *do* want our children to feel guilty when they've done wrong.

At our house lives a cat—his name is Clyde. And one cannot own a cat without providing for its needs; that is, one must have what the pet industry has designated in its admirable command of euphemism, "Kitty litter." And one cannot have a tray full of kitty litter in the same house with an insatiably curious toddler without having some remarkable adventures—adventures which, in our case, result in a great deal of sweeping up the floor and a great deal of trying vainly to explain to a 15 month old daughter why she ought to leave kitty's litter alone. Words like "dirty," "naughty," and "no, no, no" are uttered with all due emphasis and solemnity.

A few days after a major clean-up episode, my wife, Ann, and I noticed that our daughter Katie was not in the room with us. It did not take us very long to figure out where she'd gone. I tromped down the stairs to the basement with fatherly foreboding. Sure enough, there across the room with litter scattered yon and hither, stood the light of my life. She looked up, and before I could say a word, ran towards me with eyes wide, arms waving, and the words, "my, my, my, my!" which, freely translated, meant, "Oh, my goodness gracious, daddy; I wonder how all *this* happened!"

And behind my laughter formed the awareness that our daughter had begun to learn the meaning of guilt.

To experience guilt is to move toward maturity. But that's not all there is to it. For guilt often causes problems, mostly when it is not resolved, but instead lingers on, often to fester much like an untreated wound. Sometimes it remains unresolved because we may not even be consciously aware of its presence. I need not use psychological terminology to illustrate that guilt can have a harmful effect on our minds, emotions, and even our bodies. We've all heard of enough cases where guilt feelings contributed to depression, or coronary illness, or divorce, to know that feelings, even deeply buried feelings, can cause varied kinds of problems.

Guilt is an especially disruptive feeling. It can make us condemn in others the wrong we don't want to face in ourselves. It can keep us away from the very people who could help us get ourselves together again. We fail to set things right with the people we have wronged, because just being around them reminds us of our wrong.

Our guilt can lead us in another direction. We may busy ourselves in all kinds of "good works" in an unconscious desire to justify ourselves, to earn our way back to being acceptable. Or we may, again unconsciously, want to be punished for our wrongdoing, and so we set ourselves up to be clobbered over and over again. So that, often, guilt is not just the result of doing wrong but the long, drawn-out extension of wrong doing.

We can get caught in a vicious cycle. We do wrong and that makes us feel guilty so we do wrong again and that makes us feel more guilty, and on and on it goes.

What is the way out of all this; what is the answer to guilt?

There is no easy answer, and those who suggest there is make it doubly difficult for the person feeling guilty. For one thing, getting rid of guilt is not something we can accomplish on our own. As Frederick Buechner writes, "It is about as hard to absolve yourself of your own guilt as it is to sit in your own lap."

The Christian faith makes the assertion that the answer to guilt is found in the gracious forgiveness of a loving God. Central to the New Testament faith is a conviction expressed pointedly in the book of Titus:

> ... when the goodness and loving kindness of God our Savior appeared, he saved us, not because of deeds done by us in righteousness, but in virtue of his mercy ... (Titus 3:4-5).

What this means is that the initiative for the removal of guilt comes

THOU SHALT NOT STEAL

from God himself. He reaches toward us, willing the brokenness we feel to be replaced by wholeness. We do not have to prove ourselves to God, regain his confidence or his love. We need not, and in fact, cannot, disguise the sinfulness in our lives. We need only come to him, just as we are, and receive his blessing.

How does this happen? What does it mean to say God receives us with our guilt? All too often, such a statement remains a vague abstraction to the one in need of forgiveness. How can it become a living reality?

In the New Testament we read how divine forgiveness became real in the form of a person. The story in Mark's gospel of Jesus healing a paralytic speaks to us because it is so personal, so human (Mark 2:1-12). We don't know what caused the man's paralysis. All we are told is that those who brought him to Jesus went to great lengths to get their friend into the Master's presence. They went up on the roof, made an opening, and lowered the pallet on which the paralyzed man lay.

I've always wondered why Jesus said what he did to the paralytic. Mark tells us that his words were: "My son, your sins are forgiven." There's no mention that the man asked for forgiveness. No doubt he had come to Jesus to be healed, to be given the power to walk. If he had made a request, it probably would have been something like: "Master, strengthen my legs; let me walk and run like other men."

But Jesus, looking at him, said, "My son, your sins are forgiven." With the gifts of understanding and perception he had received from his heavenly Father, Jesus could tell that this man's deepest need was the need for forgiveness. Perhaps the paralytic's feelings of guilt had been so deeply buried over the years that he no longer was in touch with them. Maybe what really paralyzed him was the sense of unworthiness he carried with him wherever he went. But hearing the words of this rabbi, who by merely looking at him seemed to know all about him—the best and the worst—the paralyzed man felt accepted, forgiven. And so he was ready to hear and believe when Jesus said to him, "Rise." The man picked up his bed and walked. Forgiveness was possible because God spoke through the Christ.

What about our own time? Jesus doesn't walk the streets of our town as he did centuries ago in Palestine. How can we experience the taking away of our guilt?

The answer again is that God works through people. To borrow another thought from Buechner, in order to feel truly forgiven, we need somebody in whose presence we can put aside our disguise, trusting in that when he or she sees us for what we truly are, our friend won't run away screaming with either horror or laughter. In such a person's presence the fact of our guilt no longer makes us feel and act out our guiltiness. For a moment, at least, the vicious circle stops rotating and we can step down onto the firm ground of acceptance, where maybe we'll be able to walk a straight line again.

Keith Miller tells of an occasion when a young woman was conversing with him about the possibility of making a Christian commitment. She said that a personal problem made it impossible for her to become a Christian. Miller moved easily into his best "witnessing" style. He told her that Christianity is called "goodness" because God invites us all into his family, no matter what our life has been. What follows is Miller's own account:

> "But," and she hesitated. . . . "I don't feel acceptable until I whip this problem."
>
> "Listen, Susan, the old song doesn't say, 'Just as I am when I whip my major problem,' It says, 'Just as I am without *one plea,* one *promise,* or *guarantee.*'"
>
> She looked at me with the strangest dawning look of hope, "Do you really believe that?" she said.
>
> "I'd bet my life on it."
>
> She looked down at her hands for several minutes. "All right," she said, almost as a challenge, "I'm committing adultery every Thursday night with a man who has a wife and several young children. And I *cannot* quit. How can I come into your Christian family?"

Miller then recalls that his first reaction was a stunned one, for he had not expected her to say anything like that. His conditioned response was to suggest that perhaps she was not ready for Christ, at least until she cut down on this offense.

But then he realized how phony we Christians are:

> Of course we would expect her to quit committing adultery. We don't mean "just as I am without one plea." We actually mean, "Just as I am when I promise implicitly to straighten up and quit my major sins." And this girl had nailed me with her honesty.

She had heard the hard, unyielding demand of the church and knew she didn't have the strength to quit "sinning." Yet it was that need, her weakness, that had prompted her to seek Miller's (and the church's) help. Miller tells how he dealt with it:

I thought about Jesus and what He would have done. Then I looked up at her. "Of course, you can commit your life to Christ just as you are," I smiled. "He knows you want to quit seeing this man, and I don't know where else you can ever *hope* to find the security and strength to break up with him. So if your commit your life to Christ right now, then Thursday night, if you find you can't help meeting your friend, take Christ with you in your conscious mind through the whole evening. Ask Him to give you the desire and the strength to break off the relationship."

And she stepped across the stream and became a Christian.

(From *Habitations of Dragons,* by Keith Miller, WORD Book Publishers, 1970.)

The good news of the Christian faith is that God accepts us just as we are, that we need not carry our guilt forever. Just as the woman in Keith Miller's story found freedom and courage, so can we step across the stream of our fear and experience the acceptance that God offers us.

And we too can find new life.

GOBBLE-UNS, DEMONS, AND THE GOSPEL

What comes to your mind when you see the word "demonic"? Maybe you are reminded of the stories in the Gospels of Jesus casting out unclean spirits; maybe you bring to mind such movies as "The Exorcist"; or "The Omen"; maybe you have no vivid impressions at all when you see the word.

For me, the word "demonic" stirs up memories of dark, cold winter nights, with the wind howling outside and rattling the window panes. In a few more minutes it would be bedtime. Time remained only for one last story. Hearing the wind and catching the mood of the moment, my dad would begin his recitation of an old favorite, guaranteed to make even grownups shiver a little. What it did to us kids is beyond imagining.

> Little Orphan Annie's come to our house to stay,
> An' wash the cups and saucers up, an' brush the crumbs away,
> An' shoo the chickens off the porch, an' dust the hearth an' sweep,
> An' make the fire, an' bake the bread, an' earn her board-an' keep
> An' all of us other children, when the supper things is done,
> We set around the kitchen fire an' has the mostest fun
> A-list'nin' to the witch-tales 'at Annie tells about,
> An' the Gobble-uns 'at gits you
> EF YOU DON'T WATCH OUT!
>
> Onc't they was a little boy wouldn't say his prayers —
> So when he went to bed at night, away up stairs,

His Mammy heerd him holler, an' his Daddy heerd him bawl,
An' when they turn't the kivers down,
HE WASN'T THERE AT ALL!
An' they seeked him in the rafter-room, an' cubby-hole, an' press,
An' seeked him up the chimbly-flue, an' ever'wheres, I guess;
But all they ever found was thist his pants and' roundabout—
An' the Gobble-uns'll git you
EF YOU DON'T WATCH OUT!

(*Little Orphan Annie*
by James Whitcomb Riley)

When I hear the word "demonic," I think of the goblins—unknown, unseen powers that could suddenly reach out and "get me."

But, you may object, that's only a carry-over from childhood. How is it possible for intelligent men and women to believe in the existence of demonic powers?

That is a very important question—one that deserves a thoughtful, honest answer.

It's certainly true that our understanding of the world has changed drastically since biblical times. People in Jesus' day had no knowledge of things like bacteria and viruses. They had no scientific understanding of what causes earthquakes or drought. They could not explain in psychological terms the factors which caused persons to lose their minds.

Lacking this kind of knowledge, they relied upon intuition and imagination to supply answers to their questions about the evil in the world around them. They spoke of evil spirits, demons which had the power to take possession of a person's mind and to infect a human body with disease. They gave names to these demons, and they believed the strongest of them was a fallen angel named Satan.

Belief in beings known as demons persisted for centuries. It was only with the coming of the scientific age, in the seventeenth century, that Western civilization began to dispense with the need for such an idea as the demonic. Philosophers and scientists taught that the only reality in the world was matter. Since matter could be examined and experimented with, it became possible to explain things like catastrophe and disease.

So it was that demons and devils came to be regarded as the superstition of primitive religion. People began to believe in progress as a guaranteed process in human experience. Given enough time and

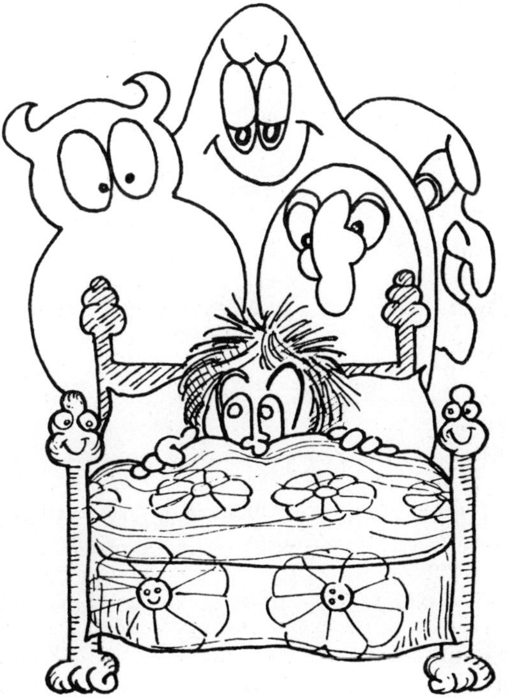

know-how, the human race would overcome evil in all its forms. There was no need to believe in demonic forces.

Then came the twentieth century. Suddenly the bright dreams of inevitable progress went up in smoke. It was the smoke of a war that stretched across all of Europe. Then came the smoke ascending from the incinerators of Nazi concentration camps and finally the ultimate horror: the smoke of mushroom clouds over Hiroshima and Nagasaki.

What had happened to peoples' confidence in their ability to make the world good? What was the source of the terrible violence let loose upon the world? People saw that, like the personalized demons of past ages, greed and hatred could take possession of the human mind. They could generate force enough to overthrow institutions, demolish cities, and fill the air and water with poison.

You and I live in a time when once again it is possible for intelligent men and women to believe in the existence of demonic powers.

However, unlike the people of a previous age, we do not think of the demonic in concrete, personalized terms. We do not picture in our minds little human-like figures with barbed tails, horns, and pitchforks. No, our experience is that of nameless, faceless forces that invade the human scene and then withdraw again, so swiftly that they cannot be identified.

And when they leave, we do not know where they have gone. Where do the demonic powers of war exist in time of peace? Where do we point to the forces of inflation and recession that constantly threaten our economy?

Nowhere and everywhere.

What terrifies us most about the demonic is its stealth, its invisibility. We cannot know how and when it will attack us next. Where in that huge crowd is the face of the assassin who, with one bullet, can strike down the President and plunge our nation again into horror and grief? Who of our friends or loved ones will next fall victim to the silent killer named "cancer"? What unspeakable force is it that comes over us and puts ugly words on our lips—words that hurt the very people we love?

We do not know. We cannot know.

The words of the Apostle Paul take on a frighteningly accurate meaning when he writes in Ephesians:

> Our fight is not against human foes, but against cosmic powers, against the authorities and potentates of this dark world, against the superhuman forces of evil in the heavens (Ephesians 6:12 NEB).

And the goblins we feared in childhood turn out to be real enough after all!

What does our Christian faith have to say to all this?

It makes a bold assertion. It says in uncompromising language that as terrifying as are the demonic powers in league against us, they cannot and will not stand against the power of God. That good news is demonstrated most vividly in the life, death, and resurrection of our Lord, Jesus Christ.

During his brief ministry, Jesus frequently cast out the demons that possessed the people who came to him. He had a greater power to draw on than the demons had. And the climax of the story comes with a cross and an empty tomb.

If you have ever doubted the existence of the demonic, if you have ever wondered whether evil is a reality in this world, then you have not taken seriously what happened on that lonely, bleak hill called Calvary. For it was there, one dark day, many years ago, that all the forces of evil came together in one massive, obscene effort to win a final victory. All the demonic powers that lodge in human hearts, in the seats of political power, in the very universe itself, threw their worst at him who was God's chosen one.

For a brief time it looked as though they had won. Is it any wonder that the sky turned black and the earth trembled and human hearts failed? But only for a moment. In Christ, God challenged the powers of darkness, took the worst they could muster, and displayed that he was stronger than they. We Christians believe that in Christ God has disarmed the demonic powers. It is only a matter of time until the force they exert will be destroyed completely.

Do you see how this changes things for us?

We know how it's all going to come out. The demonic powers still threaten us, still cause us pain and grief; there is no denying that. But we know they are living on borrowed time. Where once we believed that sin and death and evil were invincible, we now see their power is an illusion.

In fact, it is precisely as an illusion that they have terrorized humankind from the beginning. They whisper in our ears that status and wealth and power are the really important things in life. They tell us that peace of mind and security can be found in material possessions. They insist to some of us that capitalism and democracy are the only salvation for the human race. And to others of us they insist that only through Communism can the world be set right. To all, they proclaim that violence is the way to win.

In these and countless other ways do the demonic powers exert control over our minds. Their weapons are suspicion and fear and deceit. They urge us to follow them, to believe them. And many do. Many, many do.

We, who belong to Christ, dare not.

We are called to a higher destiny. We have higher orders to follow. We stand under a greater Protector than all the demonic powers put together.

With Paul we say, "If God be for us, who can be against us?"

With Paul we declare:

> I am convinced that there is nothing in death or life, in the realm of spirits or superhuman powers, in the world as it is or the world as it shall be, in the forces of the universe, in heights or depths—nothing in all creation that can separate us from the love of God in Christ Jesus our Lord (Romans 8:38-39 NEB).

This is our hope, unshakable and steadfast.

This is our faith.

BRINGING IN THE . . . WHAT?

The harvest.

For many Americans living today, that word "harvest" brings to mind a picture of huge mechanized monsters gobbling their way across huge golden fields of wheat. The great machines do it all—cutting the stalks, tearing the kernels from them, sending the straw one way and the grain itself to storage bins. It's all done with speed and efficiency.

But this modern version of the harvest has been with us only a few short decades. Before modern machinery came along, harvest time was a process virtually unchanged since those long-forgotten days when a man first learned that grain ground into a meal could keep his family alive. And, of course, there are still a great many parts of our world where the grain harvest is done the primitive way—cut by hand, gathered into bundles or sheaves, and then beaten by flails to free the precious kernels of wheat.

As a small boy, I was fortunate enough to get one of the last glimpses of a harvest tradition which preceded the mechanized operations of today. For most of the first seven years of my life, we were tenants on land owned by a Mennonite farmer. Conservative in his outlook, he had chosen not to invest his money in the newfangled machine called a combine. Instead he and his sons relied on the old way of harvesting wheat. Two horses pulled a mechanical device simply called a "binder." It cut the stalks and pulled them together into a sheaf. A man sitting on the binder tied the sheaf with twine and then it was tossed to the ground. Other men followed after and stacked the sheaves into neat piles called shocks.

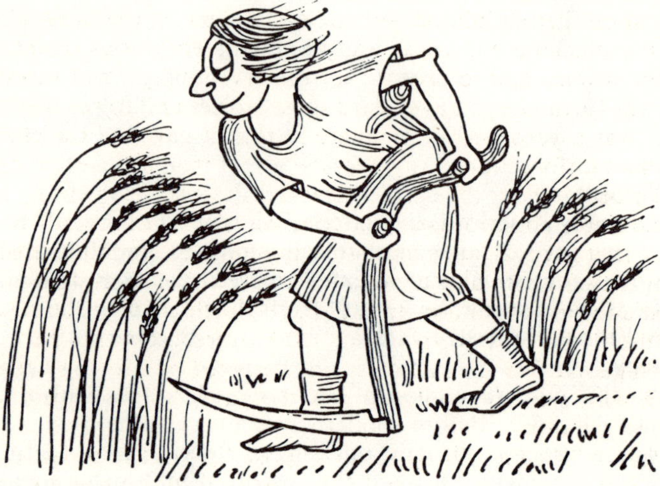

But the real excitement was still to come. On threshing day, a huge, noisy contraption was hauled onto the barn floor. This was the threshing machine. Powered by a steam engine, the threshing machine required about a dozen men to run it. Some threw the sheaves into the opening which resembled nothing so much as a huge, voracious mouth. Others bagged the grain; still others piled up the straw which the machine spewed out. And the sounds were a delight—horses neighing, men shouting, the steam engine chugging, the threshing machine itself grinding, thumping, squealing, whirring, and banging. It was a wondrous, a thrilling show for a seven-year-old.

I knew harvest time was a great event. My mother had told me stories about her childhood—of the excitement on the farm when the threshing machine had come and about the enormous quantities of food the women had to prepare for the ravenous gang of threshers.

I was fortunate to have heard these stories and to see these sights when I was a youngster—fortunate in that it gave me the chance to learn in an unforgettable way a lesson about man's close and dependent relationship with the earth. I learned there was something important and noble about the struggle to wrest from the land a living. The sight of that gang of workers—straining muscles, sweating profusely, gulping down water and lemonade—drove this lesson home. And I learned another lesson too. In the prayers offered at mealtime and at the church where we worshipped, I discovered that this partnership between people and the earth was one designed by a loving Creator. It was he who sent the sunshine and the rain, he who provided the bountiful harvest.

Many of the favorite texts of our preachers had to do with earthy, agrarian themes: Jesus teaching about the birds of the air and the lillies of the field; Jesus telling a story about a selfish rich man whose harvest was so large that he decided to tear down his barns and build bigger; the Apostle Paul using farming terms to explain how he had planted the seed of the gospel, someone else had watered, but God had given the increase; Paul explaining that unless a grain of wheat falls into the earth and dies, there is no hope of a harvest.

It's not at all hard to understand why so much of the Bible speaks directly to men and women who live close to the land. The Bible is a most earthy book. It was from one of the Psalms, Psalm 126, that one of the great American gospel hymns was taken. The last four lines of the Psalm were the inspiration:

> He that goeth forth and weepeth,
>   bearing precious seed,

shall doubtless come again with rejoicing,
bringing his sheaves with him.

So it was that country folk loved to sing *Bringing in the Sheaves:*

1. Sowing in the morning, sowing seeds of kindness,
Sowing in the noontide, and the dewy eves;
Waiting for the harvest, and the time of reaping,
We shall come rejoicing, bringing in the sheaves.

CHORUS: Bringing in the sheaves, bringing in the sheaves,
We shall come rejoicing, bringing in the sheaves.

2. Sowing in the sunshine, sowing in the shadow,
fearing neither clouds nor winter's chilling breeze;
By and by the harvest, and the labor ended,
We shall come rejoicing, bringing in the sheaves.

3. Go then, ever weeping, sowing for the Master,
Though the loss sustained our spirit often grieves;
When our weeping's over, he will bid us welcome,
We shall come rejoicing, bringing in the sheaves.

Nowadays, most people probably don't even know what "sheaves" are. But to a farmer, bringing in the sheaves was indeed a time of rejoicing.

I have said the Bible is an earthy book with a natural and direct appeal to those who live close to the land. But, of course, the Bible is not a farmer's almanac. It deals with matters that extend beyond the cycles of the seasons, the natural order of seedtime and harvest. The Bible speaks of God and his ways with his creation. It speaks of humanity—the heights to which it can rise and the depths to which it can sink. And so, while the biblical writers may use words and illustrations drawn from rural life, these words and illustrations point beyond themselves to things of a universal, even eternal significance.

When the Bible uses imagery relating to harvest time, it does so primarily for two purposes. One is to issue a warning. The other is to offer a challenge.

Let's consider the first of these purposes. Harvest time is always the climax of the farmer's efforts. It is the end towards which he has been working. It is the culmination of his labors. And in just this sense do the biblical writers use the imagery of the harvest to refer to the end-time, to the close of the age, the finality of things. Nearly every time the Bible speaks of final things, it includes a strong note of warning. The end-time will be that time when all accounts will be settled. That which has been hidden will now, finally, be brought to light. The just receive their due reward; so do the unjust.

It is the very nature of God to be a just and righteous God. Our popular concept of justice is a figure holding up a balance scales and having the eyes blindfolded so as to show no partiality. But the Christian idea of justice is the all-seeing eye of God. He is the eternally righteous one; no act of love or deed of unkindness escapes him. He knows not only the deed, but the motivation behind it. And in his good time, he will set all things right.

How much there is in life that strikes us as being unfair. We read about an injustice done to a man sent to prison for a crime he did not commit. Years later his innocence is proved, he is released and the state tells him how sorry it is. But who can give him back those wasted years? No one. How unfair, how unjust.

We hear of a young girl with a great future ahead of her. She is a brilliant student, the pride of her parents, the joy of the young man she will soon marry. Suddenly she is struck down by a rare disease. She goes into a coma. And after a long time of existing in this half-human state, she dies. And we think: "How terribly unfair!" This is but a natural, human response.

Our faith, however, teaches us that ultimately justice will come. Jesus tells the story about the farmer who sows his field. At night, the enemy comes and sows weeds in the field. It's impossible to pull out the growing weeds for fear of uprooting the wheat. What shall be done? Wait until harvest time. Workers will be sent out to reap the weeds, tie them into bundles, and throw them into the fire. Others will bind the wheat, and the grain will be stored for food (Matthew 13:24-30).

God, in his own time and his own way, will set things right. Ultimately there is victory over those evils which plague us, such as catastrophe, disease, and injustice.

The Bible also has another use for the picture of bringing in the sheaves. It is one of challenge. The Gospels tell us that Jesus had been going through the towns and villages of Galilee, and on the way he was preaching the good news, or as the Anchor Bible translation puts it, "proclaiming the freedom of the kingdom."

A part of this message is the healing of the diseased and infirm. Then the text says something which points to the essential nature of the man from Nazareth.

> When he saw the crowds, he had compassion for them, because they were harassed and helpless, like sheep without a shepherd (Matthew 9:36).

"When he saw the crowds, he had compassion for them."

What a revealing statement. There are some persons in human history who are able to draw large crowds of people. They may be politicians or war heroes or religious leaders. They stand up and urge their listeners to do this or that and their words stir the people, move them. Have you ever wondered what the feelings of such gifted speakers are towards the people they are addressing?

I would guess that the great majority of them are hoping to advance their own cause. They may fear the crowd, or enjoy the attention of the crowd, or they may despise the crowd for its mindless enthusiasm. But it can rarely be said of one who addresses crowds of people that "he had compassion for them."

In his uniquely compassionate way, Jesus turns to his disciples and gestures to indicate that he is talking about the crowd that has gathered:

> The harvest is plentiful, but the laborers are few; pray therefore the Lord of the harvest to send out laborers into his harvest (Matthew 9:37-38).

It may be that what I've been discussing has seemed to you rather out of touch with the world in which you live. It is interesting to read about old-time wheat harvests, with their sheaves and shocks and threshing machines, and it is interesting, in a quaint sort of way, to learn how the Bible uses harvest imagery. But what does all this have to do with our lives? What relevance is there to Jesus telling his disciples, nearly 2,000 years ago, that the harvest is plentiful, but the laborers are few?

I believe the words of Jesus ring as true today as they did when he first spoke them. Surely, in our day, the harvest is plentiful. The needs of the multitude are great, as varied as are faces in a crowd. And we need to see ourselves as a part of that potential harvest, for we have needs. We have problems and hangups that make us long to hear the good news of God's freeing love. We have guilt that needs forgiving; we have sorrows that need comforting; we have doubts that need answering; anxieties that need quieting; brokenness that needs healing; personal demons that need to be cast out.

We are part of that crowd on which Jesus has compassion. We are always part of that crowd, always part of that field "white unto harvest." And that's why we go to worship, that's why we are part of the church. Not because we are better than our neighbors, but because we recognize our need—the need of God's saving, forgiving, freeing love made visible in Jesus Christ.

But if we are always a part of the wheat ready for harvest, that is not all of it. We are also, and *at the same time,* one of those to whom the call comes to be laborers. "Pray the Lord of the harvest to send out laborers into the harvest." The need for that prayer still exists.

You know the suffering in our world today. You are aware of the millions who haven't food enough to survive. You know of the many lonely people in your community. You know there are men and women in prison who are angry and bitter because no one seems to care anymore. You know there are people enslaved by all kinds of enslavement: greed, prejudice, alcoholism, poverty.

You and I are not called to save the world, either individually or collectively. But we are called to find our place in the corps of laborers which our Lord sends into the field. You and I are called to respond to the needs which our talents and energy and resources fit us for.

We are part of those fields which need harvesting, and we are laborers called to the harvest.

Not one or the other; but both at the same time.

THE CHRISTIAN'S GUIDE TO GOOFING OFF

Neither the human body nor the human mind can do without periodic refreshment. The need for sleep demonstrates this fact. As far back as history goes, there are records of festival days and holy days which provided a break in the daily round of hard work. The Hebrew people discovered that human need for rest was one of the basic laws of God. Hence the fourth commandment:

> Remember the Sabbath day, to keep it holy. Six days shall you labor, and do all your work, but the seventh day is a Sabbath to the Lord your God; in it you shall not do any work" (Exodus 20:8-10).

The fourth commandment relates to a primary human activity—work. Work is the principal means of staying alive, and for centuries work has been closely related to the immediate needs of the family—killing game, harvesting crops, making clothes, preparing food. But work has acquired new meanings. It becomes a way of identifying ourselves. We are known as insurance agents, secretaries, homemakers, teachers. By pursuing our work with diligence, enthusiasm, and pride, we may gain approval from our peers and a sense of well-being for ourselves. Then too, one of the greatest benefits of work is the chance it gives us to serve humanity. Work in this sense is a privilege, a gift from God.

Yet, like all God's gifts, work can be misused. Many people regard work as a universal good, as the panacea for individual maladjustment and social crisis. What is the average American's solution to the problems of the young, the poor, and the minorities? "Find them jobs, make them work"—as though the process of work itself was a means of salvation. That idea may be a kind of Americanized theology, but you will not find it in the Bible.

What the Bible does teach is that any object, idea, or activity can become a false god. Somehow, work has gotten mixed up with the Christian religion so that many church people regard work as a worthwhile end in itself. Many of us think that not to be working is itself sinful. We find it hard to relax on a free day, to kick off our shoes and just goof-off. Something inside nags at us to do something: read a book or nail some boards together—anything so long as it keeps us busy.

It's time we wise up. This compulsion to activity that disguises itself as a Christian virtue is no such thing. Work saves no one from sin, death, or the power of the devil. In fact, work can, and often does, become the center around which a person's life revolves. Work can also become the standard by which we measure a person's value. In both such cases, work is used sinfully. True enough, work as a sin is an eminently "respectable" one—seldom as noticeable as alcoholism or larceny—but a sin it may be, all the same.

One can argue that there are genuine rewards for the man or woman dedicated to work. But sometimes the rewards are dubious ones. Those who take their work most seriously are often penalized (though they wouldn't call it a penalty) by being promoted to positions that require them to work even harder. And the extra money they make, they are expected to use to raise their standard of living. That means buying things.

And when we buy things, we have to spend time using them. For example, a family decides to purchase a snowmobile or a camper, reasoning that it will be a wholesome form of recreation. Either one of these items is a significant investment of dollars. And what American, having spent hard-earned money, will not try to get the dollar's worth by using the new equipment as much as possible?

Now using a camper takes time. It may take some of the family's work time, but more likely it will cut into their non-work time—their "free" time. Thus the more leisure-time products a family buys, the more time and energy they will devote to using them and the less truly "free" time they have left.

So it is that leisure and work become almost indistinguishable. And the refreshment and renewal that we need so badly remain only a deferred, unfulfilled hope.

How can leisure be used creatively to accomplish that renewal of

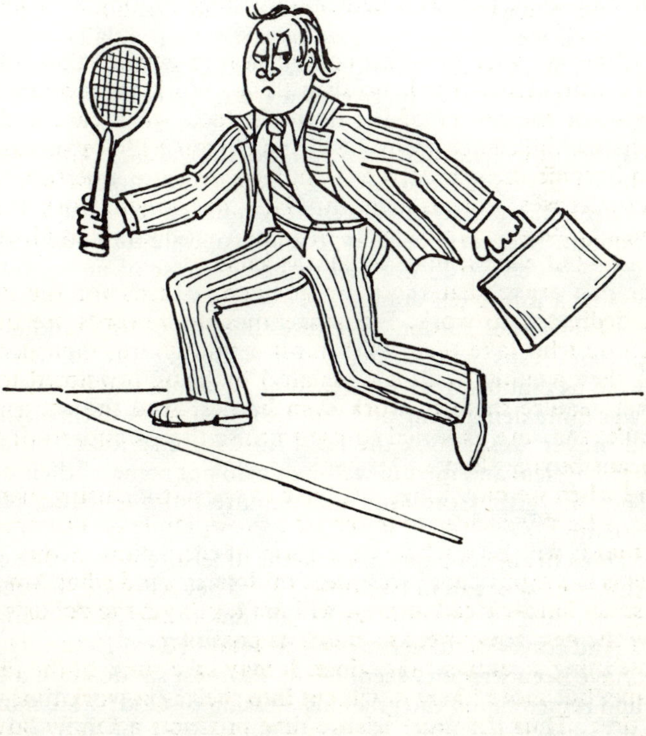

ourselves which God wills? We can begin by recognizing the spiritual dimensions of leisure.

By spiritual dimensions I mean simply that the process of refreshment to the human spirit is essentially a gift from God—a gift that can be developed and made more beneficial. Consider for a moment some of the elements of Christian worship. People worship God for many reasons, but one of them has to do with a desire to gain strength for the days ahead. I have heard many people say that activities of daily living take their toll on them and they find worship in God's house a great restorer of both faith and emotional well-being. This happens because in worship we put ourselves into God's hands. We ask him to forgive us for the wrongs we have done and for the good we have left undone. Then we ask God to give us strength for daily tasks. And finally, as we listen to his Word, we feel that God does indeed care for us, that he has the power to give us a fresh start. In worship we are remade.

It is certainly true that one can worship almost anywhere and under almost any circumstances. Yet it is certainly much easier to worship in surroundings that are reasonably quiet so that distractions are at a minimum. In a very real way, the appropriate time for worship is leisure time—when we do not feel rushed because of an appointment to be kept or a job to get done.

It was this combination of leisure time, quiet surroundings, and worship that Jesus sought many times during his ministry. The Gospels tell us that his work of preaching, healing, and just being with people was quite demanding and that he found renewal through seclusion and prayer. Jesus took the need for leisure seriously because he knew that physical and mental well-being do not come of their own accord. They are gifts from God that require times of being ready to receive them.

This idea of the religious dimensions of leisure is found also in the Old Testament. We read in Isaiah 40:31, "They who wait for the Lord shall renew their strength, they shall mount up with wings like eagles." And consider the setting of the beloved 23rd Psalm. How else could it have been written except as the Psalmist sat down in a time of leisure and remembered the gracious blessing of God? "He makes me lie down in green pastures. He leads me besides the still waters; he restores my soul. He leads me in paths of righteousness for his name's sake." How beautifully those words describe how God intends us to find restoration in our leisure time.

Yet we give ourselves too few of such opportunities. The crazy thing is, we suppose that driving ourselves, keeping constantly on the go, is somehow virtuous. From my own personal experience I know what a perverse pleasure ministers can get by letting people know how busy they are.

"My goodness, Pastor Jones, I don't see how you find time to get all your work done. You're always on the go."

"Oh, not really. Why just two weeks ago I had an afternoon off."

Ministers are not the only ones with this problem. We all make constant references to the lack of time for this or that activity. We deny ourselves leisure because it makes us feel important to let our friends know how constantly in demand we are. And when we do take some time for ourselves, we feel good about it only if there is something to show for it afterwards: "Well I broke a hundred this time out on the golf course"; "I did manage to get some sun this afternoon"; "I got half finished with that new book I'm reading."

All of this—the whole set of games we play—is more often than not just plain sin. After all, it is sin to think we don't need restoration of mind and body. The Hebrews knew this. They said that even God himself, after six days of creation, finally rested on the seventh day. Somehow, we miss the message of that.

Is it time we learn to let God renew us in times of leisure? Let me briefly suggest three ways we can prepare ourselves for it.

First, we can guarantee periods of leisure. Usually what we do is tell ourselves we'll take a break if we have time left over after work. Not surprisingly, such leftover time rarely materializes. For those of us who need help in finding time for leisure, we ought to schedule it. Sounds strange, maybe. But we schedule the rest of our time, don't we? If times of renewal are vital—and they are—they should be scheduled too. Otherwise they just don't happen.

A second suggestion: take some of your leisure in relative solitude. It's true that social gatherings can be both fun and relaxing, but how few times we truly get away from interruptions. If possible, stay out of range of the doorbell, the tv set, and the telephone. One who advocated solitude was Henry David Thoreau. In his words, "We meet at very short intervals, not having had time to acquire any new value for each other." There is wisdom in that statement. And in our leisure time spent in solitude, we are free to think of things we normally neglect. Our relationship to God, for instance. Quiet times of meditation, reading of inspirational literature (especially the Bible), prayer . . . all of these can allow God to refresh us wonderfully.

A third suggestion is this: don't try to justify time spent at leisure—either to others or yourself. If golf is a balm for your jangled nerves—enjoy it; don't feel you must improve your score every time. If you enjoy reading and sleeping in the sun—do it without apology and without justifying it as a way to get a tan.

We need to discover that goofing off during leisure time is nothing to feel guilty about. It's actually a way God can use to give us laughter and joy and inner peace.

LOVE YOUR BODY

What do you suppose Adam (the very *first* Adam) thought when he got his first good look at himself? There weren't any mirrors back then, of course, so no doubt it wasn't until he saw his reflection in a clear lake that Adam had any idea what his whole body looked like. And Adam, being the very definition of what was human, probably responded to that first glimpse of himself in much the following manner:

> "So, there I am.
> I'm not a bad looking sort, really.
> Good set of choppers. Nothing nearly as good as the teeth on that tiger though. Pleasant enough looking face. Of course, I'm hardly what you'd call a beauty. Sure is a lot of skin showing too. Golly, I've got less hair than any of the creatures. It would have been nice to have a warm woolly coat like the sheep or to be dressed in the beautiful red feathers of the cardinal. And as for strength, well, I can lift rocks and carry them, but I sure don't have the muscle power of the elephant or the pulling strength of the horse. And this body of mine is so slow. Almost any creature can outrun me; in a race with the cheetah I feel like I'm standing still. Lord, are you sure this is what you had in mind for my body? Any chance of trading it in on a new model?"

Now that imaginary soliloquy of Adam's may have seemed silly to you. And you're right, of course. It was silly. Just as silly as some of the thoughts you and I have had about our own bodies.

The adolescent years are an especially trying time for us humans, because it's then we become acutely aware of our bodies. We feel and see physical changes taking place, and what we observe can cause some intense anxiety.

During my late adolescence I was unfortunate enough to suffer from virulent attacks of acne. And if ever in my life I thought the Lord had botched a job, it was when I thought about the slip-up in quality control he had made in letting my broken-out face off the production line.

How I envied my friends, they of the blemish-free complexions. How I dreaded the job of trying to shave off my newly-sprouting whiskers, whiskers strategically placed, by some malevolent power, among the unwelcome eruptions on my face. Trying to use a razor blade in such circumstances was to flirt with unintentional suicide from loss of blood. And whereas my non-pimpled friends considered their wallets to be the most valuable possession worn on their persons, I thought differently. If, in a crowd, I suspected pickpockets lurking about, my hand instinctively darted to that tube of Clearasil in my pocket, which was both constant companion and balm in Gilead.

I suppose all of us have had times when we doubted the Almighty's judgment in designing our bodies. There's probably not a person in the world who is perfectly content with his or her body. While men wish for broader shoulders or better arches on their feet, women long for longer lashes, tresses that are darker (or lighter), more of themselves at some places and less of themselves at other places. And this state of affairs continues throughout life. If anything, it gets worse the older we get—our hair changes color or it departs altogether; we begin to experience aches, pains, and diseases which remind us that our bodies are running down, getting old, wearing out.

And even in our advancing years there are people to envy. We wish we could be in the same good condition as that of our neighbor who's exactly our age, but whose body seems ten years younger than our own. We see a picture in the paper of a 90-year-older who goes for a swim every morning and jogs a mile each afternoon. And we think to ourselves: "Why is it that I've never been truly happy with my body?"

That question has troubled human beings at every time in history. One way of dealing with it has been to devalue the body, to regard it as unimportant, or at best, a nuisance. Of importance in church history was a philosophy quite widespread in the first centuries of the Christian era. This philosophy was known as Gnosticism, and it held that only the realm of the intellect and the spirit were important. The merely physical was to be despised. Christians who were attracted to

Gnostic philosopy began to teach that Christ had not really been human; he only looked human. They believed the human body was too corrupt for God ever to appear in such form.

But the New Testament writers repudiated the Gnostic view. So in John's Gospel we read: "The Word became *flesh* and dwelt among us" (John 1:14). And the Apostle Paul did not accept the Greek view that at death the soul is freed at last from the body which is its prison house. Paul believed that when we leave our physical bodies behind we are given a "spiritual body" (1 Cor. 15:44). Exactly what this "spiritual body" was like, Paul did not say. But like the other biblical writers, Paul subscribed to the Hebrew understanding that the human body was an important part of God's creation, that like everything else in creation, God saw that it was "good." Genesis says, "God created man in his own image" (Genesis 1:27). And the phrase, "in his own image," refers to the *totality* of "man." In Hebrew thought, this means the self, the personality, the whole person.

Therefore we discover that the Bible, far from regarding the body as corrupt or despicable or insignificant, actually teaches that the body is to be honored as an indispensable element of a good creation. Martin Luther was reflecting this view of the human body when he said, "The fact that Adam and Eve walked about naked was their greatest adornment before God and all creatures."

Coming across that quotation from Luther, I was reminded of the humorous scene in the movie *Oh, God!* where the Lord comes into the bedroom of Jerry, the man God has chosen as his messenger. Jerry is taking a shower at the time, and he is embarrassed at the thought of stepping out of the shower without any clothes on. Sensing his embarrassment, God says to Jerry, "What's the matter? You think I don't know what you've got?" Although that's a somewhat mundane way of saying it, that line from the movie is in perfect keeping with the biblical understanding of the human body. God shaped us, and felt good about it when he finished.

Thus we do well to take a fresh look at the feelings we have about our own bodies. True, neither your body or mine is perfect, exactly as we might wish it could be. But on the other hand, our bodies are not merely nuisances which get in the way of the really worthwhile things of life. Like so much of what we have, our bodies are gifts — gifts from God. The important question for us ought not be, "Why isn't my body stronger or more beautiful than it is?" but rather, "What will I do with this gift I have from God?"

As with all gifts, we can either neglect and abuse the gift of our body or we can offer it in service to our Lord.

Let's consider the first option. The abuse of the human body is nothing new but it seems to have reached new extremes in our day.

In some sense, we can speak of a "neo-gnosticism" today. Recall that gnosticism was a philosophy which downgraded the physical in favor of the spiritual. One evidence of this old idea in modern form came with the growth of the drug subculture of the 1960s. Learned professors and their disciples began advocating the use of drugs in the quest for spiritual enlightenment. The effect these drugs might have on the body was considered inconsequential in relation to the spiritual truth to be gained. For the most part, that kind of "trip-taking" has been discredited, but one result of the whole movement was an aura of respectability given to drug-taking. It came out of the back alleys, onto the college campus, and into the suburban living room.

In reality it was nothing more than a sophisticated version for the same tired old reasons people have always given to justify their usage of every kind of drug—alcohol, nicotine, "nerve pills," caffeine. "It helps me relax." "It makes me feel more at ease in a social setting." "It helps me get more work done." We've heard them time and again; we've used them ourselves; and we conveniently ignore the statistics which tell us that every drug, to a greater or lesser degree, produces harmful effects on the human body.

Another way in which we often abuse the gift which is our body is in the matter of diet. And here it's not so much a matter of deliberately choosing to consume what we know to be harmful as it is habits formed out of ignorance. Our living patterns have changed in the last few decades: more and more we eat so-called "convenience" foods, the pre-mixed, pre-cooked, instant foods adapted to suit our busy schedules. Convenience is one thing; good nutrition is something else. Most of us are not eating very well. Our diets are high in sugars and fats and preservatives. Without knowing it perhaps, we are mistreating our bodies and those of our children.

But enough emphasis on the negative. For there is another choice we have instead of mistreating the body, we can offer it to God "as a living sacrifice," to use a biblical phrase (Romans 12:1).

It is obvious that the work we can accomplish, whether its purpose be that of providing for our own or our family's needs or of doing acts of good will and helpfulness to our neighbors and loved ones, is dependent to a large degree on our bodily strength. So good health is not just something that's nice to have for its own sake, it is requisite for the fulfilling of our calling as Christians.

Paul, writing in 1 Corinthians, went a step further. He asserted that our bodies were temples in which God's spirit could dwell. As Christians, we are free to do anything we choose, said Paul. But not all things we choose are helpful; some of our choices can enslave us.

Our bodies are limbs and organs of Christ himself (1 Cor. 6:12-20).

So what we use our bodies for should honor Christ. We cannot separate physical acts from the rest of our activity. What we do with our bodies will have psychological and spiritual consequences. And the opposite is true as well. Our mental and emotional state affects our physical well-being.

We know this to be true in our own experience. But usually we never go beyond an intellectual acknowledgement of this truth.

To commend a more ambitious step, I want to encourage you to start *loving* your body. That may sound strange to you. It may even strike you as repugnant. If that is so, then it's because we've been brought up to admire only the bodies of the beautiful people; the lithe, tanned limbs of the young Adonises and Venuses on the tv and movie screens.

But I'm not talking about envious admiration of some ideal. I'm talking about learning to love your own body—flat feet, myopic eyes, warts, wrinkles, and all!

Love it for the miracle it is—a flesh and blood machine of incredible resilience and adaptability, an organism so complex that medical doctors are so baffled by it far more often than they're willing to admit.

Love it because you've been through a great deal with it in your lifetime.

Love it and forgive it for the times it has kept you in bed with a wretched cold or the flu.

Love it because it has held up remarkably well considering how you've treated it.

And love it because it is God's gift to you, and it is the place where his Spirit may dwell if you will allow it; and from that dwelling place, the Spirit may smile with your eyes, may speak lovingly with your voice, may offer the hand of friendship and love.

How will you love your body? By caring for it, by treating it with respect, by not placing unreasonable demands on it. God will bless your care, for he has given you this body to serve you and to *be* you during your lifetime on this earth. And I believe—though, like Paul, I cannot begin to prove it—that when our lives here are ended, God will have another kind of body waiting for us.

And although I've learned to be reasonably happy with the body I have now, I have a feeling that my next body is going to be something greater than I can imagine.

So will yours!

MAKING BELIEVE

"Let's go to the movies!" someone says—and off you go for an evening of entertainment. What happens when you get to the movie theater? You go in, buy some popcorn maybe, find a seat, and wait for the show to start. Soon the lights go down, the curtain rises, and you are pulled into another world—a world colorful and exciting, filled with fascinating people. For the 90 minutes or so that the movie runs, that world is the one you live in.

Now the thing which makes such entrance into another world possible is the human imagination. Because you *know* those figures up there on the screen aren't real people. And you know those figures aren't really moving at all. You are aware that a great many still photographs have been taken and that when they're run rapidly through a projector, the *illusion* of movement is given. If you would stop to analyze the whole business, if you insisted upon treating things literally, you would miss the fun of enjoying the movie. You've got to make believe in order to enjoy it.

In the field of drama there is a term used to describe what happens when people go to the theater. It's called the "willing suspension of disbelief." Children call it, "making believe." I prefer the children's term and I also happen to think that "making believe" is one of the prime ingredients of the Christian experience.

Running throughout the scriptures and teachings of the Christian faith, there is an unmistakable element of "as if." And unless you and I understand this "as if" element, unless we're willing to "make believe" for all we're worth, we're going to miss out on the excitement and joy at the heart of our faith. The Apostle Paul frequently resorts to making believe in his use of creative imagery. Writing to the Colossian Christians, Paul urges his friends to remember that since their baptism they have come to a new way of life. "You were buried with Christ in baptism, in which you were also raised with him through faith in the working of God, who raised him from the dead" (Colossians 2:12).

But of course Paul doesn't mean those opening words to be taken literally. What he means is that when we are baptized, it is *as if* we are buried; and when we emerge from the water, it is *as if* we are raised from the dead with Christ. What a meaningful symbol baptism can be for us; but we won't appreciate its full significance and its beauty unless we see the "as if," unless we're willing to make believe.

Frederick Buechner has written about holy communion in terms of the "as if" attitude Christians should take to this sacred meal. To paraphrase his thoughts:

> It's make believe. You make believe that the one who blesses the bread and the cup is not the stringbean pastor who smells of Aqua Velva, but Jesus of Nazareth. You make believe that the tasteless biscuit and Welch's grape juice are his flesh and blood. You make believe that by swallowing them you are swallowing his life into your life and that there is nothing on earth or heaven more important for you to do than this.
>
> It is a game you play because he said to play it. "Do this in remembrance of me." Do *this*.
>
> Play that it makes a difference. Play that it makes sense. If it seems a childish thing to do, do it in remembrance that you are a child, and that he said, "Unless you become as little children, you cannot enter the kingdom of heaven." (From *Wishful Thinking*, by Frederick Buechner, Harper and Row).

Some people don't have much time for the Christian faith because, as they say, it's not realistic. They regard faith as an illusion, and the rituals of faith as foolish, futile exercises. I feel sorry for people who think like that, because they suppose that life is at its best when it's stripped of all elements of make believe. How barren and solemn such a life must be. Surely there is make believe in the Christian faith; if there weren't, it would be intolerably dull and lifeless. Rather than take away the make believe of our faith, I propose that we become more aware of it and enter into it with childlike abandon. And note this: making believe is not restricted to symbols like baptism and communion; it has to do just as surely with the way we live.

Again, consider what Paul writes. He tells his friends to "put to death" what is earthly in them—things like immorality, impurity, and evil desire. That is, they are to rid themselves of these tendencies, "as if" they were putting them to death. "Do not lie to one another, seeing that you have put off the old nature with its practices and have put on the new nature" (Colossians 3:9-10).

That's a statement just filled with make believe. But it goes right to the heart of Christian ethics. All of us who have committed ourselves to Christ know that the old nature (call it *human* nature, if you like) still has its hold on us, no matter how much we wish it were otherwise. Despite our best intentions, we feel ourselves pulled into doing things and saying things we know are unworthy of our best selves. But the point is that we not use that fact as an out. How easy it is to excuse ourselves by appealing to human nature.

"I'm sorry I lost my temper, but after all, I'm only human."

"Sure, I know I ought to stop smoking, but everybody is entitled to a few vices."

"I realize I acted rather stubbornly yesterday, but that's the way I was brought up; that's just the way I am."

We make such excuses nearly every day, and to do so runs contrary to the way of Christ. Paul would say to us, as he did to his Colossian friends: "Yes, I know your old human nature still clings to you. But don't use that as an excuse. Rather live *as if* you had the new nature which your faith in Christ offers."

It just won't do for us to use the same tired old alibis everybody else does. We are rightly indignant when we read about a man under the influences of alcohol committing a violent crime and getting off with a light sentence because he claims he "wasn't responsible." Our excusing ourselves on the basis of our weak human nature is essentially no different. As Christians, we are called to live as if we had a totally new nature. The early Brethren sometimes said it like this: "We must live as if the kingdom of God had already come in its fullness." To take that attitude is to make believe for real!

What kind of make believe does this require? I think the best model is the kind of make believe youngsters engage in. Watch children playing with dolls or playing "go to the store" or pretending to be Superman. They know they're making believe— they know the doll isn't really a baby; the big carton isn't really the check-out counter at the supermarket; the cape they're wearing doesn't really make them Superman. They know it's make believe—but that doesn't stop them from throwing themselves wholeheartedly into the fun of what they're doing. That's the secret of the kind of "as if" life the Christian should lead.

Now certainly such a style of life leaves us vulnerable to the perennial criticism of church people by outsiders—that of hypocrisy. I

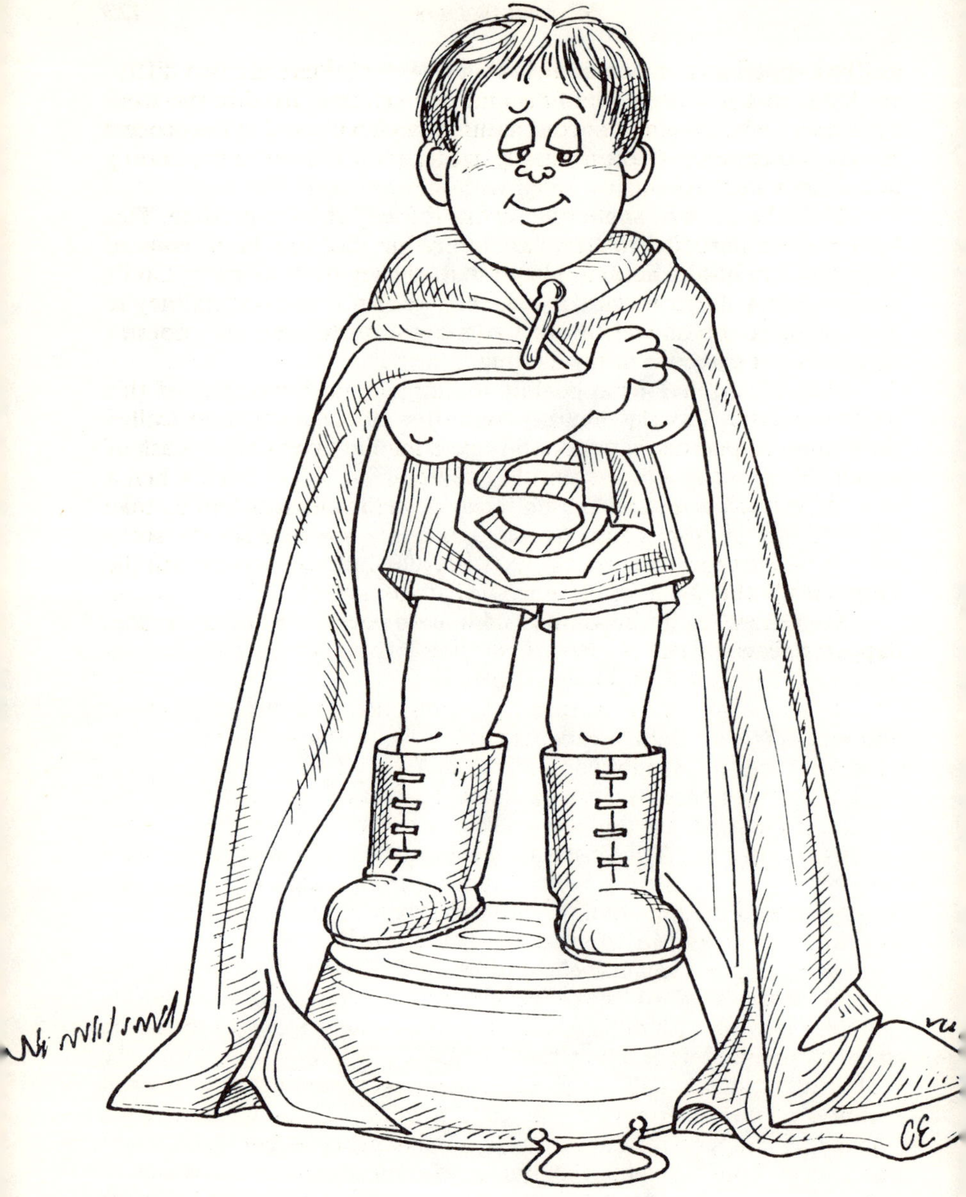

dislike hypocrites as much as anyone, but I think there are two different kinds of hypocrites. The first kind are genuine, dyed-in-the-wool hypocrites, who pretend to be something they aren't and in the process convince themselves that they really are as good as they're pretending to be. Only they aren't.

The other kind of hypocrite is what I'm urging us to become. This kind make believe their old human nature has died and been replaced by a new Christ-like nature. They act as if they were living in God's new kingdom. Deep down they know they're not as good as they're pretending to be and cheerfully admit as much, but that doesn't dampen their enthusiasm for making believe.

Now it's strange what sometimes happens to hypocrites of this second variety. Max Beerbohm tells a story about a character called the Happy Hypocrite. It's about a wicked man who wears the mask of a saint to woo and win the saintly girl he loves. Years later, when a cast-off girlfriend discovered his scheme, she challenges him to take off the mask in front of his beloved and show his face for the sorry thing it is. He does what she suggests only to find that underneath the saint's mask, his face has become the face of a saint.

My fellow happy hypocrites, that's what may, by God's grace, happen to each of us.